MORE FiSH MORE VEG

MORE FiSH
MORE VEG

Tom Walton

murdoch books

Sydney | London

INTRODUCTION

Some people are a little nervous about cooking fish. There's all this talk about being careful not to overcook it, otherwise it tastes like rubber – but not undercooking it, either. It can all feel very daunting, and makes cooking seafood sound like an exact science, which is so far from the truth.

Cooking fish isn't difficult, and you definitely don't need to be a chef to pull off a perfectly cooked dish. My advice is not to shy away from cooking fresh fish; it all starts with great ingredients – the fresher, the better. And, ideally, try to use sustainable, locally sourced seafood.

I want this book to be both an inspiration and a guide to use every day, but also for when you want to flex or indulge in something special. This is *your* book now, and I'd love you to make my recipes your own; to swap fish for veggies or vice versa. Or maybe it's winter and you want to cook a recipe from the summer chapter; I encourage you to recreate it using winter produce – be open and fluid. The beauty of vegetables and seafood is that they pair so well with a bounty of flavours. These recipes (or guides) are only here to get you started.

A little bit about me ...

I grew up in the Blue Mountains in NSW, where I was lucky to live next door to Nadeema, my Lebanese neighbour. She became like a grandma to me and as soon as I could walk, I was with her in her garden and kitchen. It was here I was immersed in Lebanese food and culture, as well as in gardening. I learned early on about cooking with the seasons, using what we had and what was at its best. It taught me how to be flexible with traditional recipes, and how to adapt them using what was available.

We would travel to Granville in western Sydney to stock up on za'atar, spices, fresh Lebanese bread, lamb and coffee. In the garden, I would plant and harvest the corn, tomatoes, cucumbers and lettuce. We grew apricots, plums, oranges, pomegranates, figs, lemons, chillies, walnuts and, of course, an abundance of herbs to make tabouli. We would pick edible weeds to make salads and pies. We would often prepare fresh *kibbeh* and *kibbeh nayeh*, toum and hummus, and we would make the most intoxicating babaganoush over a small coal barbecue.

Good Friday was always a big day for Nadeema and her family – it was when they would make vegetarian versions of all the meat dishes they loved. There was also always plenty of fish and, of course, fresh chips cooked in olive oil.

It was during these first 17 years of my life that a love of cooking was instilled in me; not cooking like a professional chef, but cooking to share and to nourish my family in our kitchen, the most important kitchen of all. This was also when my passion for vegetables, spices, acids – and for balancing and clashing flavours – was cemented. Recently, I've found myself unlearning a lot of what I was taught in the commercial kitchen and going back to those earlier years, to find where I am most content. It's inspiring to share all of this and to see it resonate with so many people.

When I was 16, my passion for food took a huge leap forward when I fell in love with Japanese food. The Japanese respect for and restraint with ingredients – especially fish – really resonated with me. I've always loved fish. I would book myself into Japanese seafood cooking classes at the Sydney Fish Market and my parents would drive me there and back. I learned to prepare sashimi, bonito, sushi and pickled fish dishes. The more I stepped towards the food world, the more it pulled me in.

At 19, as a second-year apprentice chef, I began taking part in cooking competitions across Australia. I ended up cooking my way to the world stage, where I represented Australia in Helsinki over four days of intense cooking, competing with chefs from 24 countries. This fresh-faced boy from the Blue Mountains came third in the WorldSkills cooking competition. I had taken a six-month break from my apprenticeship to train and compete. The experience taught me a lot about myself and tapped into a part of my brain that I could unlock for creativity, whether it was with a humble bag of carrots or the freshest seafood. It's a creativity I still lean on today – only now, my filing cabinet is bigger.

During my food journey over almost two decades in the industry, I have immersed myself in so many different cultures and kitchens. The way I see it, there are many connections to flavours that have formed throughout history – myriad ingredient combinations and a diversity of dishes that were built around necessity and what was available at a certain time and place. We try to label these as different cuisines, but I just see them as different connections to deliciousness, all of which tell a different story. And we are all free to tell our own, so please use my recipes as a launchpad to adapt as you like.

The dishes I share these days combine the open mind and palate of my travels with my career in food, my time as the father of young kids cooking simple yet flavourful meals for my family, a confidence with ingredients and a passion for health and wellness. The latter has been a journey that is underpinned by balance – it's not defined by a single meal, week or month. For me, healthy eating is an approach that embodies deliciousness, abundance, and cooking and eating with the seasons, with as little interference as possible.

EAT WELL,
TOM

HOW TO USE THIS BOOK

The recipes in this book are a selection of my favourite dishes featuring fish and veg. For the purely veg-based recipes, look for the 'Goes with' symbol, which provides suggestions of fish or seafood pairings so you can mix and match according to your preference. On pages 26–35, I've included basic instructions on how to cook different types of fish, so you'll have a few techniques up your sleeve, whatever you buy.

I wrote this book in the hope it would be helpful, versatile and inspiring. You'll find its pages filled with suggested variations to appeal to different palates and dietary needs. If you don't have a certain herb or vegetable on hand, or you don't like the ones I've suggested, simply swap them for something you do have, or leave them out entirely. That's where these recipes become your own – this is your book, so get it dirty!

At the back of the book I have included a chapter called the Arsenal of Flavours (see page 219), my go-to selection of flavour-packed sauces, dressings and marinades. When a recipe calls for something from the arsenal, make that first and then integrate it into the recipe. You can often prep these well ahead to save time. The whole point is to arm yourself with a fridge or pantry full of flavour weapons, to make your cooking simpler and much more delicious.

LOOK FOR THIS SYMBOL FOR FISH AND SEAFOOD PAIRINGS

Goes with

My pantry staples

Acids (vinegars/citrus juices): I love bold flavours that are often unbalanced in the classic sense of the word. While a conventional ratio for dressings would be 1 part acid to 3 parts oil (1:3), I often use a ratio of 1:1 or 1:2, and I sometimes use a blend of vinegar and citrus. I love how this lifts dishes and provides a foundation of flavour. My favourite vinegars are sherry vinegar, chardonnay vinegar and apple cider vinegar.

Olive oil: I use a lot. Where possible, I like to stay away from vegetable oils. I use olive oil to cook with, and a good extra virgin olive oil to dress salads, vegetables and to finish a dish. This is for a combination of health and flavour reasons. This is how I cook, but I don't want to make your kitchen more complicated or expensive, so if you find a good quality all-rounder that is local to your area, feel free to use that across everything. Otherwise, if you want to have a nice finishing olive oil, try some different varieties – there are some amazing producers out there creating oils with such varied characteristics.

Salt: When it comes to seasoning or finishing a dish, salt will always be number one in my kitchen. I use good-quality sea salt flakes. Don't be scared of using salt, especially if your diet is low in processed foods. But again, adjust according to your personal taste and needs.

Black pepper: I use a lot of this, too. For me, black pepper is an important ingredient and I like it to stand out in a dish. Recipes in this book that call for chilli will often use less or no black pepper.

Goods, store bought: I'm all about normalising things that make life easier and don't impede on results. **Canned legumes** are what most of my recipes call for – they're what I use at home and I encourage you to do the same. **Frozen peas** are also great. **Store-bought pastry** is a godsend. The key message here is to celebrate these shortcuts if they're going to encourage you to create and share a beautiful meal while alleviating some time and stress.

Tahini: If you follow me on social media, you'll know that tahini is one of my biggest food loves. It is one of the most versatile ingredients you can have in your pantry. I couldn't include everything I love to make with it in this book, but I share a lot on my socials, so keep an eye out. Tahini transcends Middle Eastern cuisine – it can be a base for Asian dressings or stirred through soups for a finishing flavour bomb. It's also amazing drizzled straight over fresh tomatoes. I prefer hulled tahini, and quality is everything – not all tahini is created equal.

Other favourite pantry items

- Cumin seeds
- Ground coriander
- Caraway seeds
- Sweet smoked paprika
- *Ras el hanout*
- Curry powder – I love a good-quality butter chicken curry powder
- Za'atar – The best quality ones are from Middle Eastern delis or specialty online spice shops
- Calabrian chilli in oil, or a good-quality chilli oil

- Pepitas (pumpkin seeds)
- Sunflower seeds
- Nuts
- Pomegranate molasses
- Tamarind concentrate
- Black vinegar
- Rice vinegar
- Sesame oil
- Soy sauce or tamari

CHOOSING FISH AND SEAFOOD

SUSTAINABILITY

I couldn't write a book celebrating fish and seafood without addressing the important question of sustainability. To help untangle the ever-changing, complex world of seafood sustainability, I've collaborated with writer and food critic Ant Huckstep to provide this snapshot of the current state of play.

In its simplest form, fish sustainability is about ensuring that the environment, habitat and co-inhabitants of both farmed or wild-caught seafood do not come to harm. Just as important as the sustainability of each particular species is the sustainability of the towns and families who, over generations, work with Mother Nature to protect both the species and their livelihoods.

So how can we navigate all this as consumers? It's a tough balancing act. The subject of seafood sustainability is complex, so it's important to listen to the scientists.

In Australia, we have some of the strictest-managed fisheries on the planet. The scientists at the Fisheries Research and Development Corporation (FRDC) work in consultation with fisheries agencies to monitor fish stock density, to help create real-time quotas and to ensure the ongoing sustainability of stocks.

You don't need to strap yourself to a ship to become an eco-warrior. Small, easy adjustments to everyday life can have a huge impact on sustainability. Where possible, try exploring different varieties of fish, which might mean buying a species you haven't cooked before. Soon enough, you will fall in love with fish seasonality, much like the way we love stonefruit or asparagus season.

It also pays to choose quality over quantity. Over time, we have adopted the mindset that a large piece of protein and a small side of vegetables is the norm, but it's much healthier and more affordable to eat smaller serves of protein and up your veg intake. By using better quality produce and less of it, you're also using less packaging and, therefore, reducing waste. So you're not only creating a greater awareness and connection to your food, but you're leaving a smaller footprint and leading a healthier lifestyle, too.

Sustainability is a journey, not a destination. The more you care about what fuels your body, the easier it is to live a more sustainable lifestyle.

A note on seasonality

In Australia, we are blessed with some of the world's most amazing fish and seafood. However, the question of how to enjoy eating it sustainably without depleting stocks is one that we as consumers now face as we make our purchasing decisions. While we have many well-managed fisheries in Australia, there are still issues with over-fishing some species. One way to address that is to think about the concept of seasonality when it comes to seafood.

Like vegetables, seafood has broad seasons, where availability of certain species differs depending on the climate. If we apply this seasonality ethos when we buy fish, we won't rely too heavily on one or two species, and instead try a greater variety of fish all year round. Eating a greater variety of seafood isn't just better for the planet – it's good for our health, too.

In the recipes in this book I suggest a range of available seafood, both wild and farmed, for each season. This is not set in stone as each region will have different conditions that affect seafood availability, so use this as a guide and feel free to swap for other available species. The flavours and ingredients are designed to be versatile and adaptable to help you do just that. In this way, you will hopefully feel confident to try new species and eat a wide range of seafood throughout the year. The more we talk to fishmongers and come to understand the seasonality of seafood, the more sustainable our seafood choices will be.

Nine steps to a better connection to food sustainability

1. Shop from a trusted source whenever possible

Find a fishmonger you can trust, and begin a conversation to discover what may be in season and particularly good at that time. Asking the simple question, 'what's great right now?' at the fish counter, as well as letting them know you are interested in trying what's at its best, is very powerful.

You can, of course, buy great seafood from supermarkets, too. The key to buying quality seafood from supermarkets is to look for sustainability accreditation, as many stores only stock seafood that carries these credentials. When shopping, look for seafood that glistens, looks fresh and has no aroma other than that of the sea.

Be brave, open-minded and prepared to try a species you may not have cooked before. The more you start doing this, the more you'll begin to broaden your repertoire and knowledge and – most importantly – your confidence. There are so many recipes in this book you can interchange and there are so many species that can be substituted in each recipe.

2. Do some basic research

There are many excellent resources available. One of my favourite books on the subject is the *Australian Fish and Seafood Cookbook*, an incredible deep dive into the world of Australian seafood and one I reach to all the time for inspiration. In the UK, Mitch Tonks' *Fish: The Complete Fish & Seafood Companion* does the research on your behalf and celebrates the seasons beautifully, while a must-read in the US is Barton Seaver's *American Seafood*.

There are also great online resources out there to help us better understand our seafood. The FRDC website has incredible detail about species, seasons, harvesting methods and sustainability. Doing a little bit of research and arming yourself with knowledge before going shopping is a great way to navigate the world of seafood sustainability.

3. Look for local seafood wherever possible

Looking for certain labels that represent responsible fisheries can be helpful, but not paramount. For example, while there is still much room for improvement, both Australia and New Zealand have some of the most strictly managed sustainable fisheries on the planet. Both countries also have the most spectacular species, and a level of care that is unmatched. The UK and US have a lot of accredited fisheries, and a lot of small fisheries where seasonal catch is at the heart of their operations.

Ultimately, it comes down to gaining confidence to buy in-season species that you may not have previously tried. It may mean you need to step out of your habits, but if you undertake to purchase seafood of the highest quality, you can be sure of the utmost level of care from catcher or farm, to market. Those producing the highest quality are innately concerned with the sustainability of the species and the fishery.

Be mindful that the stock density and status of every species is different all over the planet. A fishery or farm in one part of the world may be the most sustainable of its kind, and yet in other places, its sustainability might be in question, so ensure you investigate before casting a wide net. Take salmon, for instance: in Australia, we farm Atlantic salmon, which GoodFish – Australia's sustainable seafood guide – says no to. I choose to cook New Zealand king salmon, a slightly different species that is farmed to world's best practices by Ora King Salmon and Mount Cook Alpine Salmon. Our choices when purchasing fish influence good practice and quality, and the more we get this part right, the more we can ensure there is plenty of fish tomorrow and long into the future.

4. Look for healthy fish

Whole fish stays fresher longer and allows you to check the quality markers: eyes should be clear and plump, aromas should be clean and fresh like the sea, scales should have a consistent covering, and the fish should be covered in a clear, clean protective coat of natural fresh 'sea slime'. If you don't have the confidence to fillet a whole fish, buy it whole anyway, and ask your fishmonger to fillet it for you. If you're buying fillets, look for those with a fresh, clean aroma, a bright sparkling colour and a translucent sheen.

5. Shop with seasonality in mind

This can be a minefield, because we have access to seafood from all over the world, and different seasons arrive at different times across Australia. So always ask where your seafood comes from, or check the label if buying from the supermarket. But when a fish is in peak season, it is abundant, cheaper and the quality will be second to none. This means it works with your budget, it's not impacting stock density and you will be enjoying the fish or seafood at its optimum.

6. Spend more time immersed in the food world

If you want a better understanding of where your food comes from, get as close to the source as you can. I'm not suggesting you knock on the gate of a farm, but try to visit a fish market or a farmers' market and speak to the people closest to the source. Often, especially when it comes to farmers' markets, it's the producer, catcher or farmer sharing their crops or catch. Knowing more about how your food is grown, where it's grown or how it's caught, can give you a better understanding of its impact on your health, how to cook it and how you are fuelling your body.

7. Try to buy whole fish every now and then

Famous British chef Fergus Henderson put the notion of nose-to-tail eating on the map. Sure, he didn't invent it, but he inspired a generation of chefs and consumers to respect the whole animal, and showed them just how delicious secondary cuts and offal can be. Utilising the whole fish is no different. You don't need to eat eyeballs, but whole fish is, in fact, really simple to cook and generally more affordable. It's also a little more forgiving – the spine acts as a heat conductor and the fats along the spine help keep the flesh moist. And if you're thinking about sustainability, using every part of a whole fish is very important. You can use the bones for a broth, the head can be split and grilled – there are so many uses that are simple and delicious. If fish butchery is not your thing, ask your fishmonger to fillet a whole fish for you, but ask to keep the bones and head to make stock, which forms a tasty base for so many meals.

8. Cook simply and with variety

When it comes to food, simplicity is one of the most spectacular things. When you use quality ingredients, all you need is to choose the technique that helps them shine on the plate. A less-is-more approach means the palate won't get confused by too many flavours, so you can really appreciate the produce. The more you cook with variety, the more you understand the versatility of ingredients. When it comes to fish, eating the same species over and over is not very sustainable. There are so many wonderful types of seafood – the more you mix it up, the less impact there'll be on specific fisheries and the greater the benefits to your health.

9. Start a small garden

Not everyone has a green thumb, but growing a few things at home – even a small balcony garden with tomatoes, herbs and perhaps something easy like silverbeet (Swiss chard) – is a great option. When you have herbs on hand, or you experience the stages of a tomato from seed to blushing red beauty, there is a sense of joy and satisfaction in achieving a goal with the most delicious reward. And, if dipping your toes in the deep blue takes your fancy, give fishing a go and head straight to the source yourself!

My top fish and seafood

We've grown accustomed to celebrating the seasonality of vegetables and fruit, and we've learned to realise the value of a product in its peak condition. The same principles apply if you want to enjoy seafood at its very best. Here is a list of some of the seafood I love to cook with, which are sustainable, affordable, versatile and, most importantly, delicious. Most are available year-round, due to the varied water temperatures and seasons across Australia and New Zealand. And if you buy them in their peak season, they'll be abundant and at a better price, too.

Blue-eye trevalla

Peak season: Winter.
This is one of my all-time favourites. Blue-eye has a white, mild, super-meaty flesh. It's delicious roasted, pan-fried, poached, char-grilled or barbecued. It holds up to big flavours just as well as it does to lighter ones.
Substitutions: Bass groper, bar cod, blue warehou, hapuka, pink snapper.

Blue mackerel

Peak season: Autumn to early winter.
Blue mackerel is fast-growing, affordable and abundant. It has a dark, oily flesh with a rich flavour. I can't go past barbecuing it – try it with any of my Arsenal of Flavours (page 219).
Substitutions: Bonito, trevally.

Bream

Peak season: Late summer to early winter.
Bream has a sweet, white, mild flesh and is much more affordable than snapper. It's perfect roasted whole, bag-cooked or pan-fried as fillets.
Substitutions: Deep-sea bream, pink snapper, silver warehou, tropical snapper.

Gemfish

Peak season: Winter.
Gemfish has a white, mild flesh. It has so much flavour and richness without being overpowering. It is great crumbed, roasted, pan-fried, barbecued or char-grilled.
Substitutions: Most large white fish, such as warehou.

Kingfish

Peak season: Wild – autumn to spring; farmed – year-round.
With its high fat content, kingfish really is one of a kind. Its rich, oily white flesh is delicious raw or seared, and it's great when lightly poached in a curry or skewered and then barbecued.
Substitutions: Cobia, mahi mahi, Spanish mackerel, trevally.

Leatherjacket

Peak season: Autumn to spring.
Leatherjacket is super affordable and abundant. Its flesh is mild, white and sweet, with no small bones. Try it whole or filleted, roasted, poached in a curry or grilled on the barbecue.
Substitutions: Mahi mahi, swordfish.

Ling

Peak season: Winter and spring.
Ling is widely accessible and versatile to cook with. Its firm, meaty and sweet white flesh makes it perfect for crumbing, barbecuing, or poaching in a curry. It suits almost every flavouring.
Substitutions: Blue cod, deep-sea bream, hapuka.

Mussels

Peak season: NSW, TAS and VIC – late summer to early winter; SA – winter to spring; WA – spring.
I call them nature's super food because they're sustainable, delicious, fast and simple to cook, plus their white flesh is light and healthy.
Substitutions: None.

NZ king salmon

Peak season: Winter.
Rich, pink and oily New Zealand king salmon is perfect raw, cured, roasted or barbecued. It works so well with spicy flavours, like when it's buried in my king salmon biryani (page 158).
Substitutions: Rainbow trout.

Octopus

Peak season: Year-round.
Once you learn my basic technique to prepare octopus (page 90), you're just minutes away from tender tentacles. Its light white flesh loves the light char of a barbecue – try marinating in my salmoriglio (page 224) before grilling.
Substitutions: Squid, cuttlefish.

Rainbow trout

Peak season: Year-round.
This reliable all-rounder is milder in flavour than king salmon, but still has a sweet, buttery, pink flesh. First-timers should give roasting whole rainbow trout a go.
Substitutions: NZ king salmon.

Scallops

Peak season: Tasmanian – winter to early summer; Queen – year-round; Saucer – year-round.
Buttery, sweet scallops are delicious raw, cooked quickly over high heat or grilled in their shells. Pair with an Asian dressing or a rich butter sauce.
Substitutions: None.

Spanish mackerel

Peak season: Late winter to spring.
I love the firm, oily, rich and meaty flesh of Spanish mackerel. It's perfect for char-grilling, barbecuing or gently poaching in a curry.
Substitutions: Mahi mahi, trevally, yellowtail kingfish.

Squid

Peak season: Southern calamari squid – late winter to spring.
Squid's light, sweet, tender white flesh stands up to most flavours. Grill it to caramelise the exterior and turn it smoky, or stir it through a rich ragu and serve with pasta.
Substitutions: Octopus.

Tiger prawns (shrimp)

Peak season: Farmed – summer; wild – late summer to autumn and spring to summer.
The firm, white, sweet flesh of Aussie tiger prawns is amazing. Barbecue, char-grill or poach them – minimal intervention is best.
Substitutions: King or banana prawns.

Tuna

Peak season: Yellowfin – autumn to spring; albacore – winter to spring.
Tuna is easy to prepare, whether raw, seared or barbecued. Yellowfin has a dark, rich, oily flesh, while albacore is mild, white and sweet. I love the sweetness of albacore, either raw or seared.
Substitutions: Spanish mackerel.

HOW TO COOK FISH AND SEAFOOD

SIMPLE COOKING TECHNIQUES TO USE AT HOME

The thought of cooking fish and seafood is daunting for many people, but it doesn't have to be. At home, I stick to a few key cooking methods that give amazing results every time. Just like vegetables, cooking fish and seafood allows for so much versatility, once you gain the skills and confidence that come with learning a few simple techniques. These skills will also give you the confidence to try new fish species, as you'll have a bag of tricks up your sleeve. Then you can cook whatever is in season at the time, or experiment with an underused species, which will ultimately save you money due to its more abundant availability.

Cooking in this more simple and sustainable way comes back to confidence, which you'll gain with practice. Once you've tried some recipes in the book and have a few runs on the board, use my Arsenal of Flavours on page 219 to try different flavour pairings as you cook your way through these pages. Think of it as a choose-your-own fish and veg adventure!

Apart from when herb-crusting (page 29), it's good to take your fish out of the fridge around 30 minutes before cooking to bring it to room temperature. This allows for more even cooking.

Pan-frying fillets for a crispy skin

Pan-frying with the lid on creates a gentle environment for the flesh to steam, while the skin is caramelised. The cooking time will vary depending on the fish species and the thickness of the fillet, so check as you go. The key to a crispy skin is ensuring the skin is completely dry before cooking. There are many species that are great for pan-frying, such as blue-eye trevalla, mirror dory or NZ king salmon.

STEP 1 Gently run the back of a knife down the fish's skin to release any moisture.

STEP 2 Pat the skin dry with paper towel. If you have time, let the fish sit in the fridge, skin-side up, for 2 hours to dry out further.

STEP 3 Add the oil and fish, skin-side down, to a non-stick frying pan over medium–high heat. Using a spatula, firmly press the fish down for 10–20 seconds, until the skin relaxes.

STEP 4 Cover the pan with a lid, reduce the heat to medium and cook until the flesh begins to turn opaque, 3–4 minutes.

STEP 5 Turn off the heat, flip the fish over and let it rest in the pan for 1–2 minutes.

STEP 6 Transfer the fish to a plate and keep warm until ready to serve.

Searing

This high-heat cooking technique is perfect for cooking fattier fish like tuna, Spanish mackerel, kingfish or New Zealand king salmon. It creates flavour by caramelising the fish's exterior, while keeping the centre rare. For an extra rare finish, sear one side only, otherwise sear both sides. This technique is also perfect for squid and scallops. You could also use a char-grill pan or barbecue – just make sure you oil the fish and not the grill to avoid it getting too smoky.

STEP 1 Season the fish with salt, pepper and any other spices you like.

STEP 2 Add the oil and fish to a very hot non-stick frying pan and sear for 30 seconds over high heat.

STEP 3 For an extra rare finish, cook the fish on one side only.

STEP 4 Otherwise, flip it over and cook for a further 30 seconds. Let it rest for 1–2 minutes before serving.

Herb-crusting

It's best to use thicker fish fillets for this, such as tuna, kingfish or NZ king salmon, as you want to keep the centre rare after searing it on all sides. Thinner fillets are easier to overcook with this technique. It's also important to keep the fish refrigerated until you're ready to cook it, so you're not raising its temperature too much while it's in the frying pan.

STEP 1 Season the fish. Add the oil and fish to a very hot non-stick frying pan and sear for 20 seconds each side, then refrigerate to cool.

STEP 2 Scatter chopped herbs over a piece of eco-friendly wrap. Lay the cooled seared fish on top and gently press it into the herbs.

STEP 3 Scatter more chopped herbs over the fish, completely covering it. Roll the wrap around the fish firmly.

STEP 4 Twist the ends tightly to enclose the fish, then refrigerate it for at least 1 hour.

STEP 5 To serve, slice the fish into 1–2 cm (½–¾ inch) thick pieces, then remove and discard the wrap.

Char-grilling and barbecuing

This technique is perfect for cooking smaller whole fish, thicker fillets or fish skewers (if using bamboo/wooden skewers, soak them for 10 minutes in water before use). Choose thicker cuts of firm-fleshed fish, such as gemfish, NZ king salmon or Spanish mackerel, as they are easier to handle and won't fall apart. Remove the fish from the fridge at least 10 minutes before cooking and make sure it's dry, unless it has been marinating. Cooking times will vary, so adjust the temperature for larger fish. Finally, it's important not to move the fish too often while char-grilling – only flip it when it comes away from the grill easily.

STEP 1 To avoid a haze of smoke, season and oil the fish or seafood, not the char-grill pan or barbecue.

STEP 2 Place the fish, skin-side down (if it has skin), onto a barbecue or char-grill pan that has been preheated to high.

STEP 3 Cook the fish for around 4–6 minutes, flipping it halfway. If you're cooking skewers (as pictured), ensure all sides are evenly seared.

STEP 4 Carefully transfer the fish to a plate and let it rest for 1–2 minutes before serving.

Crumbling

Crumbling lends itself to a wide range of fish, and is the perfect way to try new species. With three opportunities to add flavour – in the egg wash, in the flour, and in the crumbs – there's plenty of room to get creative. Go for skinless, boneless, white-fleshed fish fillets – ling, hake, bream, blue-eye trevalla, flathead, mirror dory or whiting. Peeled prawns (shrimp) and squid are also delicious when crumbed.

STEP 1 Toss the fish in seasoned flour, shaking off any excess.

STEP 2 Dip the fish into egg wash and coat it well, then drain off any excess.

STEP 3 Cover the fish in breadcrumbs, pressing them in well to evenly coat it. Refrigerate for at least 5 minutes so the crumbs firm up.

STEP 4 To bake the fish, coat it with oil spray and cook it on a wire rack placed over a baking tray in an oven preheated to 220°C (425°F) for 8 minutes.

STEP 5 To pan-fry, heat 1 cm (½ inch) of olive oil in a hot non-stick frying pan over medium–high heat and cook the fish for 2 minutes each side.

STEP 6 Drain the fish on paper towel or the wire rack and let it rest for 1–2 minutes before seasoning and serving.

Bag cooking

Cooking fish in a bag allows it to gently steam, giving you juicy, flavourful results, while creating a delicious broth or sauce. This technique suits fillets, whole fish and shellfish – try ling, gemfish, blue-eye trevalla, snapper or barramundi. It's always better to undercook the fish rather than overcook it, as the fish will continue to steam in the bag while it's resting out of the oven.

STEP 1 Place the fish in the middle of a sheet of baking paper with any other ingredients, oil and spices.

STEP 2 Pull both the long edges of the baking paper over the fish and fold together.

STEP 3 Roll up the ends to seal and form a pouch. As a general rule of thumb, cook a 200 g (7 oz) piece of fish in an oven preheated to 210°C (410°F) for 12–15 minutes.

STEP 4 Remove the fish from the oven and let it rest for 2–3 minutes. Carefully open the pouch and add any final herbs, spices or a squeeze of lemon juice before serving.

Poaching

Seafood loves the gentle heat of poaching. Use this method for delicious one-pot cooking, which is perfect for fuss-free, low mess, any-night-of-the-week meals. This technique can be used for curries and soups, or for poaching fish to flake over salads. Murray cod, gemfish, ocean trout and snapper are all great for poaching.

STEP 1 Bring your liquid or sauce to the boil. Season to taste before adding the fish, so you don't break the fish while stirring.

STEP 2 Gently add the fish, reduce the heat to a simmer and cook for the required time. If the fish isn't fully submerged in the liquid, cover with a lid.

STEP 3 Remove from the heat and allow the fish to rest in the liquid for a further 2–3 minutes (for smaller pieces) or 3–4 minutes (for larger pieces).

Roasting whole fish

This is a simple go-to technique for cooking whole fish. It works for fillets, too – simply reduce the cooking time by approximately half. Apply your favourite flavours, marinades or dressings from the Arsenal of Flavours (page 219). It is important to remove the fish from the fridge 20–30 minutes before cooking to bring it to room temperature. The following times are based on a 700 g (1 lb 9 oz) whole fish.

1   Make three shallow cuts down each side of the fish. If using a marinade, rub it into the fish and its cavity and allow it to stand for 30 minutes.

2   Place the fish on a baking tray lined with baking paper, season it inside and out and brush it with oil. Place any flavourings, such as lemon or herbs, inside its cavity.

3   Roast the fish for 15–20 minutes in an oven preheated to 220°C (425°F), until the flesh closest to its head (the thickest part) begins to flake away easily with a fork or small knife. Carefully transfer the fish to a plate and allow it to rest for 2 minutes before serving.

SPRiNG

Loaded spring hummus

Hummus and greens are two of my biggest loves in the food world. Piling a salad on top of the chickpea dip is, hands-down, one of the most delicious and simplest ways to get flavour and nourishment onto a plate. Serve this with some crisp baked pita or flatbread for scooping.

½ bunch broccolini, sliced into smaller lengths

Iced water

1 Lebanese cucumber, thinly sliced lengthways

1 bunch asparagus, trimmed and thinly sliced on an angle

½ cup (75 g) frozen peas, thawed

1 tablespoon capers, rinsed and drained

Finely grated zest of 1 lemon

Handful each of mint leaves, flat-leaf parsley leaves and dill sprigs

1 tablespoon chardonnay vinegar

⅓ cup (80 ml) extra virgin olive oil

1 teaspoon za'atar

100 g (3½ oz) marinated feta

Crisp baked flatbread, to serve

Hummus

1 x 400 g (14 oz) can chickpeas, rinsed and drained, reserving 2 tablespoons aquafaba (chickpea water)

1 clove garlic

⅓ cup (80 g) hulled tahini

Juice of ½ lemon

1 teaspoon sesame oil (optional)

Sea salt flakes and ground black pepper

To make the hummus, place all the ingredients in a blender or food processor with the reserved aquafaba and ½ cup (125 ml) water and blend to a smooth, creamy consistency. Adjust the seasoning and lemon juice to taste, then set aside.

Bring a saucepan of salted water to the boil. Add the broccolini and blanch for 30 seconds, then use tongs or a slotted spoon to transfer to a bowl of iced water to refresh for 1 minute. Drain well on crumpled paper towel and set aside.

In a large bowl, combine the broccolini, cucumber, asparagus, peas, capers, lemon zest and herbs. Dress with the vinegar, 2 tablespoons of the olive oil, a little salt and pepper and gently toss to combine.

To serve, spoon the hummus onto a large plate or into a shallow bowl. Sprinkle the za'atar over the top and drizzle with the remaining olive oil. Pile the salad over the top, sprinkle with the feta and serve with the crisp flatbread.

Goes with

· Grilled Spanish mackerel skewers
· Whole roasted rainbow trout
· Grilled tiger prawns or squid

Escabeche mussels on sourdough

This escabeche sauce is one of my favourites and works so well with mussels or any seafood, really. The mussels will keep for up to 4 days in the fridge, and the flavours just keep getting better. If you can, make this recipe the day before to really let the flavours develop.

2 kg (4 lb 8 oz) mussels, scrubbed

Handful coriander (cilantro) leaves

Handful dill sprigs

Olive oil, for splashing

Juice of ½ lemon

1½ cups (375 g) lemony crushed butter beans (see page 230) or babaganoush (see page 229, or use a store-bought babaganoush), to serve

Grilled sourdough rubbed with garlic, to serve

Escabeche sauce

⅔ cup (160 ml) olive oil

1 small brown onion, finely chopped

2 cloves garlic, finely chopped

2 fresh bay leaves

Generous pinch of dried chilli flakes (optional)

1 teaspoon sweet smoked paprika

¼ cup (60 ml) sherry vinegar or red wine vinegar

Sea salt flakes and ground black pepper

Place the mussels in a large saucepan, cover with a lid and cook over high heat, stirring occasionally, until they begin to open, 3–5 minutes. Remove each one from the pan as it opens. Alternatively, you can barbecue the mussels by placing them directly onto a barbecue or char-grill pan that has been preheated to high for 1 minute, or until they open. Remove the mussels from their shells, removing any beards as you go, and place them in a bowl. Set aside.

To make the escabeche sauce, place the olive oil in a small frying pan over low heat. Add the onion, garlic and bay leaves and cook until the onion softens, about 5 minutes. Add the dried chilli flakes (if using), the paprika and vinegar and stir. Season to taste, then pour the sauce over the mussels, mixing until they're well coated. Place the mussels in the fridge for at least 2 hours or overnight.

To serve, bring the mussels to room temperature. Combine the herbs in a small bowl and season with a little salt and pepper. Add a splash of olive oil and the lemon juice and gently combine.

Smear the lemony crushed butter beans or babaganoush onto the grilled sourdough and then pile the mussels and herbs on top.

Fish katsu salad bowl

Baking fish katsu is a little easier and cleaner than frying it. To give this a shattering, deep golden crunch, I pre-bake the breadcrumbs before coating the fish. This dish comes together in under an hour, however you can prep the fish katsu a day ahead and store it in the fridge. I love serving this as a simple salad bowl when I want something lighter, or with rice as I've done here, for something more substantial. Any firm white-fleshed fish works a treat.

Steamed rice, to serve

½ white cabbage, finely shaved using a mandolin or knife

12 snow peas (mange tout), thinly sliced

2 large handfuls baby spinach leaves

1 large avocado, cut into 8 wedges

4 radishes, thinly sliced

3 spring onions (scallions), green part only, thinly sliced

¼ cup (60 ml) rice vinegar

1 tablespoon sesame oil

½ cup (125 ml) Japanese BBQ sauce (tonkatsu sauce) (see Note), to serve

½ cup (120 g) kewpie mayonnaise, to serve

Fish katsu

1 cup (60 g) panko breadcrumbs

½ cup (35 g) shredded coconut

½ cup (75 g) sesame seeds

2 free-range eggs

2 tablespoons soy sauce

½ cup (80 g) rice flour

600 g (1 lb 5 oz) firm white-fleshed fish fillet, such as ling or hake

Sea salt flakes and ground black pepper

Olive or vegetable oil spray

For the fish katsu, preheat the oven to 180°C (350°F). Toast the breadcrumbs on a baking tray for 4–5 minutes, until golden brown. Transfer to a shallow bowl, add the coconut and sesame seeds and combine.

In a separate bowl, whisk the eggs with 1 tablespoon of the soy sauce and set aside. Place the rice flour in a third bowl. Cut the fish into four pieces, each around 1 cm (½ inch) thick, then season with a little salt and pepper and toss in the rice flour, shaking off any excess. Dip the fish pieces in the egg mixture, draining any excess, then roll them in the breadcrumb mixture, pressing the crumbs into each piece to coat well. Place the fish on a baking tray and refrigerate for at least 5 minutes to allow the crumbs to firm up.

Spoon the rice into four bowls and top with the cabbage and snow peas. Make a small pile of baby spinach to one side, then top with the avocado, radish and half the spring onion.

Mix the rice vinegar, sesame oil and remaining soy sauce together and set aside.

Preheat the oven grill (broiler) to high and position a shelf about 20 cm (8 inches) below the grill. Spray a wire rack with oil and place it over a baking tray. Generously spray both sides of the fish pieces with oil and place on the greased rack. Grill for 6 minutes, turning halfway through, then let them rest for 1 minute before thickly slicing.

To serve, top the rice and cabbage salad with the fish katsu, then spoon the rice vinegar dressing over the top. Scatter with the remaining spring onion and finish with the Japanese BBQ sauce and a dollop of the kewpie mayonnaise.

Note Japanese BBQ sauce, or tonkatsu sauce, can be found in the Asian aisle of well-stocked supermarkets or at most Asian grocers.

Slow-cooked beans with tomatoes and herbs

We ate this dish often growing up. It's a lesson in simplicity and how flavours develop and transform with slow cooking. I make this throughout the year and swap the green beans for zucchini (courgette), young tender broad beans, okra, eggplant (aubergine) or cauliflower, depending on what's in season. I've also added butter beans here, which makes the dish go further and turns it into something more substantial.

¼ cup (60 ml) olive oil
1 large brown onion, thinly sliced
Sea salt flakes and ground black pepper
1 kg (2 lb 4 oz) green beans, trimmed
1 x 400 g (14 oz) can crushed tomatoes
1 x 400 g (14 oz) can butter beans, rinsed and drained
Handful flat-leaf parsley leaves, roughly chopped
Handful dill sprigs, roughly chopped
Juice of 1 lemon
Garlicky whipped tahini (see page 223), or natural Greek-style yoghurt, to serve

Place the olive oil, onion and 1 teaspoon salt in a large saucepan. Cover with a lid and cook over medium–high heat for 10 minutes. Add the green beans and stir, continuing to cook for a further 10 minutes, until the beans begin to break down.

Add the tomatoes and stir through, then reduce the heat to medium. Cook for 20–30 minutes, until the green beans are soft and the sauce has thickened (it should be just clinging to the beans). If the sauce is too thick, add a splash of water.

Add the butter beans, stir and cook for a further 2 minutes. Adjust the seasoning if needed. At this point, you can cool the beans and store them in the fridge, then reheat them before serving or simply bring them to room temperature if you want to serve them cold.

To serve, add half the herbs and lemon juice to the bean mixture and stir through. Top with a good dollop of garlicky whipped tahini or yoghurt and scatter with the remaining herbs.

Goes with

· Pan-fried blue-eye trevalla fillet
· Pan-fried snapper fillet
· Whole roasted leatherjacket

'Freekeh-n' super-green salad with smoked almonds and feta

This salad is a great launchpad for building flavour and texture. Cook the freekeh and veggies ahead of time and then all that's left to do is mix and dress. You can swap the freekeh for farro, quinoa, buckwheat or even brown rice.

1 cup (220 g) freekeh, rinsed well

Sea salt flakes and ground black pepper

Iced water

2 bunches asparagus, trimmed and cut in half on an angle

20 snow peas (mange tout), trimmed

2 handfuls green beans, trimmed

2 handfuls watercress, leaves picked

½ cup (80 g) smoked almonds, chopped

Handful flat-leaf parsley leaves

2 tablespoons chardonnay vinegar

⅓ cup (80 ml) extra virgin olive oil

Handful onion sprouts (optional) (see Note)

100 g (3½ oz) marinated feta, to serve

Green goddess tahini sauce or sumac yoghurt (see pages 222, 223), to serve (optional)

Lemon cheeks, to serve

Bring two saucepans of water to the boil. Add the freekeh to one saucepan and cook for 15 minutes. Drain, cool and set aside.

Season the second pan of boiling water well with salt. Have ready a bowl of iced water and a large plate or tray covered with crumpled paper towel. Add the asparagus and snow peas to the boiling water for 30 seconds, then use tongs or a slotted spoon to transfer them to the bowl to refresh for 1 minute. Drain well on the crumpled paper towel and set aside. Add the beans to the pan for 1 minute and repeat the same blanching and draining process.

Combine the asparagus and freekeh in a large bowl, then add the snow peas, green beans, watercress, smoked almonds and parsley. Season the salad to taste, dress with the vinegar and olive oil and toss well to combine.

To serve, pile the salad onto a large platter and scatter the onion sprouts over the top, if using. Top with the marinated feta, some green goddess tahini sauce or sumac yoghurt, if you like, and a squeeze of lemon juice.

Note Onion sprouts are similar to alfalfa sprouts, but with a subtle oniony flavour. You can find them at specialty greengrocers or online.

Goes with

· Grilled ling fillet
· Roasted NZ king salmon fillet
· Pan-fried bream fillet

Serves 2 as a light
meal or 4 as part
of a larger meal

The 'Big Greek' village salad

This salad is a show-stopping centrepiece for the table, served with fish and grilled veggies, babaganoush or hummus. Or you could enjoy it as a meal in itself for two people. This recipe makes a generous amount of herbed yoghurt, which you can keep in the fridge for up to 5 days to enjoy with another meal.

As the iceberg halves are served whole, it's best to carve them up into wedges at the table. If you're eating a half all to yourself as I often do, just grab a fork and steak knife and get stuck in.

1 large iceberg lettuce, cut in half

1 Lebanese cucumber, cut into 1 cm (½ inch) cubes

1 vine-ripened tomato, cut into 1 cm (½ inch) cubes

½ cup (75 g) pitted kalamata olives, roughly chopped

¼ cup (60 ml) extra virgin olive oil

2 tablespoons pomegranate molasses

2 tablespoons za'atar

100 g (3½ oz) marinated feta

2 tablespoons dill sprigs, roughly chopped

2 tablespoons spring onions (scallions), thinly sliced

Lemon cheeks, to serve

Herbed yoghurt

½ bunch basil, leaves picked

2 cloves garlic

1½ cups (390 g) natural Greek-style yoghurt

Finely grated zest and juice of 1 lemon

Sea salt flakes and ground black pepper

To make the herbed yoghurt, place all the ingredients in a blender and blend into a smooth sauce. Set aside in the fridge.

Lay the lettuce halves, cut-side up, on a serving plate. Lightly season with salt and pepper and generously spoon the herbed yoghurt over the top so that it runs down the leaves.

Top the lettuce halves with the cucumber and tomato and lightly season with salt and pepper once more. Scatter with the olives, then dress everything with the olive oil, pomegranate molasses and za'atar. Crumble the marinated feta over the top, scatter with the dill and spring onion and serve with the lemon cheeks.

Goes with

· Grilled Spanish mackerel skewers
· Whole roasted rainbow trout
· Crumbed ling fillet

Rainbow chard, pepita and quinoa tabouli

Growing up, tabouli was always my favourite salad. We would grow everything for it at home. These days, I like to recreate its vibe with other seasonal ingredients. Feel free to swap the rainbow chard for any other leafy greens, and the quinoa can be switched with other grains or even lentils. This version is amazing on its own, drizzled with the tahini sauce or a little hummus or babaganoush.

1 cup (200 g) quinoa, rinsed

3 handfuls mixed herbs, such as flat-leaf parsley leaves, mint leaves or dill sprigs

2 spring onions (scallions), thinly sliced

¼ bunch rainbow chard, leaves and stems separated and thinly sliced

2 Lebanese cucumbers, thinly diced

½ cup (75 g) toasted pepitas (pumpkin seeds)

½ teaspoon sumac

⅓ cup (80 ml) extra virgin olive oil

2 tablespoons pomegranate molasses

Juice of 1 lemon

Sea salt flakes and ground black pepper

Green goddess tahini sauce (see page 222), to serve

Place the quinoa with 2 cups (500 ml) water into a saucepan. Bring to the boil, stirring occasionally, then reduce the heat to low, cover with a lid and cook for 15 minutes. Remove from the heat and allow to steam for 5 more minutes with the lid on, then spoon into a large bowl and allow it to cool. It's best to complete this step a little in advance, if you can.

Mix the quinoa, herbs, spring onion, rainbow chard leaves and stems, cucumber, pepitas and sumac together in a large bowl. You can prepare the salad up to this point in advance and refrigerate it until you're ready to serve, if you like.

To serve, drizzle the olive oil, pomegranate molasses and lemon juice over the salad and season it well with salt and pepper. Toss thoroughly to ensure everything is dressed well, and serve with the green goddess tahini sauce spooned over the top.

Pro tip If you love grains in salads as much as I do, it's a great idea to always have some cooked and on hand in the fridge, so that nourishing bowls are only minutes away. As a general rule of thumb, most cooked grains can be stored in the fridge for up to 4 days.

Goes with

· Grilled tiger prawns (shrimp) or squid
· Whole roasted leatherjacket
· Pan-fried snapper fillet

Grilled zucchini with charred onion, rice and herb salad

This is a delicious, simple recipe with maximum impact, thanks to the gnarly grilled zucchini (courgette) halves. You can swap the rice for freekeh, quinoa or buckwheat. My babaganoush (page 229) would dial things up again in the flavour stakes.

1 cup (200 g) basmati rice, rinsed

6 zucchinis (courgettes), cut in half lengthways

1 red onion, cut into 2 cm (¾ inch) wedges

⅓ cup (80 ml) olive oil

Sea salt flakes and ground black pepper

⅓ cup (55 g) pepitas (pumpkin seeds)

⅓ cup (55 g) sunflower seeds

½ teaspoon curry powder

⅓ cup (60 g) sultanas

250 g (7 oz) grape tomatoes, cut in half

Handful mint leaves

Handful coriander (cilantro) leaves

1 lemon

1 tablespoon extra virgin olive oil

1 cup (275 g) sumac yoghurt (see page 223)

Pomegranate molasses, to drizzle (optional)

Place the basmati rice in a small saucepan with 1½ cups (375 ml) salted water and bring to the boil. Cover with a lid, reduce the heat to low and cook for a further 6 minutes, then turn the heat off and allow the rice to steam in the pan.

Preheat a barbecue, char-grill pan or large frying pan to high.

Using the tip of a knife, cut shallow criss-crosses in the cut-side of the zucchinis, then place them into a large bowl or tray with the onion. Add ¼ cup (60 ml) of the olive oil and a little salt and pepper and toss to coat. Grill the zucchinis, cut-side down, and the onion, for around 8 minutes, turning the zucchini halfway and adjusting the heat if needed. The zucchini should be cooked but not soft, and the onion should be charred. Transfer them to a bowl to cool slightly. Alternatively, you could roast both the zucchini and onion in an oven preheated to 240°C (475°F) for 10–12 minutes.

Meanwhile, place the remaining olive oil, the pepitas, sunflower seeds and a pinch of salt in a small frying pan over medium heat and cook, stirring for 2 minutes, until the seeds are toasted. Add the curry powder and sultanas and stir through. Remove from the heat and allow to cool, then add half of this seed mixture to a bowl (keep the rest to snack on later), along with the rice, tomatoes, charred onion and herbs.

Dress the salad with the juice of half the lemon, the extra virgin olive oil and a little salt and pepper, then spoon it into a serving bowl. Top with the zucchini, the remaining lemon juice and the sumac yoghurt. Finish with a drizzle of pomegranate molasses (if using) and a crack of black pepper.

Goes with

· Grilled kingfish fillet
· Pan-fried Spanish mackerel
· Whole roasted barramundi

Fish skewers

Anything cooked on a skewer is more fun to eat. These make for a great lazy pass-around barbecue lunch, and will happily pair with any number of tasty sides in this book. When it comes to fish, this is a great way to try new types and flavourings.

If you can't find the fish types recommended here, feel free to try any in-season fish that's available. The most important thing to remember is to go for a large firm-fleshed fillet that can be easily cut into big pieces, so they don't fall apart. Ling, tuna, kingfish and large snapper fillets are all great options for skewering, as are prawns (shrimp) and scallops.

Salmoriglio swordfish and charred lemon

Cut a 600 g (1 lb 5 oz) swordfish fillet into 3 cm (1¼ inch) pieces and marinate in ⅓ cup (80 ml) salmoriglio (see page 224) for at least 1 hour. Cut 1 lemon into 12 thin slices. Thread 4 pieces of the marinated fish along with 3 lemon slices onto four pre-soaked bamboo skewers, alternating between the fish and the lemon. Grill on a barbecue or char-grill pan that has been preheated to high for around 4 minutes, turning throughout. Serve with some extra salmoriglio spooned over the top.

Gochujang and sesame Spanish mackerel

Cut a 600 g (1 lb 5 oz) Spanish mackerel fillet into 3 cm (1¼ inch) pieces and marinate in ⅓ cup (80 ml) gochujang dressing (see page 228) for at least 1 hour. Thread 4 pieces each of the marinated fish onto four pre-soaked bamboo skewers and grill on a barbecue or char-grill pan that has been preheated to high for around 4 minutes, turning throughout. Serve sprinkled with toasted sesame seeds and thinly sliced spring onion (scallion).

Smoked chilli and tamarind king salmon

Cut a 600 g (1 lb 5 oz) NZ king salmon fillet into 3 cm (1¼ inch) pieces and marinate in ⅓ cup (80 ml) smoked chilli and tamarind sauce (see page 228) for at least 1 hour. Thread 4 pieces each of the marinated fish onto four pre-soaked bamboo skewers and grill on a barbecue or char-grill pan that has been preheated to high for around 4 minutes, turning throughout. Sprinkle with toasted peanuts and serve with lime cheeks and lettuce leaves, if desired.

Pasta e piselli with scallops

Literally translating to 'pasta and peas', this one-pot dish hails from Naples, but my version isn't like Nonna makes it. I've used frozen peas here to simplify things, and I've added snow peas (mange tout) and asparagus to make it a true celebration of spring. My version is also on the table in just 30 minutes.

Salmoriglio is a herby, lemony sauce hailing from southern Italy. You can store it in the fridge for up to 1 week and use on other veggie, fish or pasta dishes.

1½ cups (210 g) frozen peas, thawed

½ cup (125 ml) salmoriglio (see page 224)

500 g (1 lb 2 oz) dried casarecce pasta

⅓ cup (80 ml) olive oil

¼ small leek, sliced

2 cloves garlic, finely chopped

½ teaspoon dried chilli flakes

1 bunch asparagus, trimmed and cut into 4 cm (1½ inch) lengths

12 snow peas (mange tout), finely sliced

24 scallops, roe and shell removed

Sea salt flakes and ground black pepper

Finely grated zest and juice of 1 lemon

Handful flat-leaf parsley leaves, chopped, to serve

Handful rocket (arugula) leaves, to serve

Place half the peas in a small food processor or blender and add the salmoriglio. Blend into a rough paste, then set aside.

Bring a large saucepan of salted water to the boil, add the pasta and cook until al dente, 9 minutes. Drain the pasta and reserve 1 cup (250 ml) of the starchy cooking water.

While the pasta is cooking, place a large saucepan over medium heat. Add 2 tablespoons of the olive oil, the leek, garlic and chilli flakes. Cook for 2 minutes, then turn the heat up to medium–high, add the asparagus and snow peas and cook for 1 more minute, until the veggies turn bright green. Add the drained pasta, the pea and salmoriglio paste, the remaining peas and enough of the reserved starchy pasta water to make a loose sauce that just coats everything.

Place a frying pan over high heat and add the remaining olive oil. When the pan is really hot, add the scallops quickly and sear one side for 20 seconds. If the scallops are thin, remove them now, otherwise flip them over and sear for 20 seconds. Working quickly, transfer the scallops to a plate.

Season the pasta generously with a little salt, black pepper, lemon zest and juice. Add the parsley and toss to combine. Serve immediately with the rocket leaves and scallops scattered over the top.

Notes If you want to keep this veggie-forward, leave out the scallops and top with grated parmesan.

I have used casarecce, a short, twisted pasta that I love, but feel free to use any pasta you like – fusilli or farfalle would both work, too.

Potato and pea salad with horseradish ranch dressing

You can prep all the components for this salad in advance and then dress it up to 30 minutes before serving, to keep everything nice and fresh. The horseradish ranch dressing is amazing drizzled over any other salads, too.

1 kg (2 lb 4 oz) new chat potatoes

2 tablespoons olive oil

½ small leek, cut in half lengthways and sliced into 1 cm (½ inch) pieces

1 cup (140 g) frozen peas, thawed

Handful mint leaves, roughly chopped

Handful dill sprigs, roughly chopped

¼ cup (50 g) baby capers, rinsed and drained

Large handful pea sprouts, or any other sprouts

Horseradish ranch dressing

½ cup (130 g) natural Greek-style yoghurt

¼ cup (60 ml) buttermilk

1 clove garlic, crushed

1 tablespoon white wine vinegar

Juice of 1 lemon

2 tablespoons store-bought horseradish

Sea salt flakes and ground black pepper

To make the horseradish ranch dressing, whisk all the ingredients together. Taste and season with more salt and pepper if needed. Set aside in the fridge.

Place the potatoes in a saucepan with enough cold water to cover them and 2 teaspoons salt. Bring to the boil, then reduce the heat to a simmer and cook for 15 minutes, until tender. Drain the potatoes, cool them slightly and cut them into halves or quarters. Set aside.

Place the olive oil, leek and a pinch of salt in a small saucepan and cook over medium heat for 3 minutes, or until the leek is soft.

Combine the potatoes, leek, peas, herbs and baby capers in a large serving bowl or plate. Pour the ranch dressing over the top, season with salt and pepper and toss well to combine. Top with the pea sprouts before serving.

Pro tip Potatoes are always better at room temperature, so for maximum flavour, leave them out of the fridge after cooking them.

Goes with

· Crumbed ling fillet
· Whole roasted rainbow trout
· Grilled swordfish or ling skewers

Grilled asparagus and butter bean salad with capers, chilli and lemon

I love asparagus season. I especially love thick, meaty asparagus spears, which are perfect for grilling to bring out all those gnarly smoky flavours. This salad is quick, simple and bursting with flavour. It's great on its own or with some babaganoush. Feel free to swap the butter beans for another legume, like chickpeas or lentils.

2 bunches asparagus, trimmed

1 tablespoon olive oil

Sea salt flakes and ground black pepper

1 x 400 g (14 oz) can butter beans, rinsed and drained

2 tablespoons capers, drained

2 spring onions (scallions), finely sliced

Handful dill sprigs

Handful flat-leaf parsley leaves, roughly chopped

2 tablespoons sherry vinegar

¼ cup (60 ml) extra virgin olive oil

1–2 tablespoons Calabrian chilli in oil (see Note)

Finely grated zest of 1 lemon

Preheat a char-grill pan or large frying pan to medium–high.

If the asparagus are thick, gently peel them and cut in half lengthways. If they are thin, skip this step. Toss the asparagus with the olive oil and season with salt and pepper. Grill for around 2 minutes, turning them throughout until lightly charred.

To assemble, place the asparagus in a bowl with the butter beans, capers, spring onion and herbs. Dress with the sherry vinegar, extra virgin olive oil and Calabrian chilli. Season with a little more salt, then gently toss and serve on a platter topped with the lemon zest.

Note Calabrian chilli in oil, or Italian chilli in oil, is available at some supermarkets, delis and specialty stores. If you can't find it, use any chilli in oil.

Goes with

· Pan-fried Spanish mackerel fillet
· Grilled NZ king salmon fillet
· Whole roasted snapper

Chickpea, tomato and herb salad with pomegranate dressing

This is such a flavour-packed bowl! Grating the tomatoes intensifies their sweetness, which is amplified further with the sweet and sour pomegranate dressing. The warm chickpeas definitely make this a 'spoon salad', so grab one and dig in!

2 cups (400 g) dried chickpeas, soaked overnight, then drained, or 2 x 400 g (14 oz) cans chickpeas, rinsed and drained, reserving the aquafaba (chickpea water) from 1 can

Sea salt flakes and ground black pepper

2 tomatoes, cut in half

⅓ cup (80 ml) extra virgin olive oil, plus extra to drizzle

Juice of 1 lemon

2 cloves garlic, finely grated

2 tablespoons pomegranate molasses

2 teaspoons sumac

⅓ cup (90 g) hulled tahini

Handful dill sprigs

Handful mint leaves

2 Lebanese cucumbers, roughly chopped

2 avocados, cut into wedges

⅓ cup (50 g) kalamata olives

1 tablespoon za'atar (optional)

Pita/flatbread, torn, to serve

If using dried chickpeas, cook for around 45 minutes, until soft and creamy. Season lightly with salt and set aside. If using canned chickpeas, place the chickpeas and reserved aquafaba in a saucepan over medium heat and cover with plenty of cold water. Bring to a simmer and cook for 3 minutes, until soft and creamy.

Grate the tomatoes, holding the cut-side against a box grater, and place in a large bowl. Lightly drain the chickpeas, leaving a little water clinging to them, and add to the tomatoes with the olive oil, lemon juice, garlic, half the pomegranate molasses and sumac. Season with salt and pepper and toss to combine.

Spoon the chickpea mixture and all of its dressing into a large shallow serving bowl. Drizzle with the tahini, the remaining pomegranate molasses and sprinkle with the remaining sumac. Scatter the herbs and chopped cucumber over the top, then top with the avocado and olives. Finish with a final drizzle of olive oil and the za'atar, if using. Serve with the torn pita/flatbread.

Goes with

· Pan-fried mirror dory fillet
· Grilled ocean trout fillet
· Whole roasted bream

Fish shawarma-style wraps

These wraps are an example of how building your arsenal of condiments can help you create layers of flavour quickly. I skewer the fish in between slices of lemon, which caramelises them into a new level of deliciousness when they're grilled.

You could also make these vegetarian by swapping the fish for cauliflower florets or diced eggplant (aubergine) that have been tossed in the *ras el hanout* marinade and roasted at 220°C (425°F) for 12–15 minutes.

600 g (1 lb 5 oz) firm white-fleshed fish, such as ling, Spanish mackerel, swordfish, gemfish or barramundi, cut into 3 cm (1¼ inch) pieces

1 tablespoon *ras el hanout* (see Notes)

Sea salt flakes and ground black pepper

¼ cup (60 ml) olive oil

2 lemons

1 brown onion, cut into 1 cm (½ inch) slices

To serve

8 small Lebanese-style flatbreads

1 cup (220 g) hummus (see page 38, or use a good-quality store-bought hummus)

3 handfuls fresh herbs, such as flat-leaf parsley leaves, mint leaves or dill sprigs

1 tomato, sliced

1 Lebanese cucumber, sliced

½ cup (135 g) sumac yoghurt (see page 223), or natural Greek-style yoghurt

⅓ cup (80 ml) zhoug (see page 224)

Soak eight 12 cm (4½ inch) bamboo/wooden skewers in water for 10 minutes.

Place the fish in a bowl with the *ras el hanout*, some salt and pepper and 2 tablespoons of the olive oil and toss to coat.

Cut one of the lemons in half lengthways and then cut each half into eight thin slices. Thread the fish onto the skewers in between the lemon slices – you want three pieces of fish and two slices of lemon per skewer. If you have time, place the skewers in the fridge for up to 1 hour to marinate.

Preheat a barbecue or char-grill pan to high. Toss the onion in the remaining olive oil and season lightly with salt and pepper.

Cook the fish for around 2 minutes each side, and the onion until it's charred and gnarly, about 2 minutes.

To serve, lay the flatbreads out, spoon some hummus onto them and top with the herbs, tomato, cucumber and the charred onion. Place a fish skewer on top, then pull the bamboo skewer out and discard. Finish with the yoghurt and zhoug, wrap it all up and dive in!

Pro tip Make the condiments and skewer the fish up to a day in advance.

Notes *Ras el hanout*, a North African spice mix, is available at well-stocked supermarkets and some grocers.

You could leave out the flatbread and serve this bowl-style, bulked up with some salad leaves or shredded lettuce.

Kingfish, blood orange and avocado tostadas

Blood oranges pop into season for a brief time in late winter and early spring, so be sure to celebrate them when they do. These crisp and zingy tostadas do just that, and will have you dreaming of those warm spring days ahead. Kingfish works so well here, and searing it is a great way to release its maximum flavour potential, but you could also use other varieties of fish, like albacore tuna or grilled Spanish mackerel. If blood oranges aren't available, just use regular ones.

6 x 10 cm (4 inch) corn tortillas

¼ cup (60 ml) olive oil

Sea salt flakes and ground black pepper

250 g (9 oz) kingfish fillet, skin removed

2 avocados

Juice of 1 lemon

Handful roughly chopped coriander (cilantro) leaves, plus ½ handful whole leaves extra, to serve

3 blood oranges

¼ red onion, thinly sliced

Preheat the oven to 210°C (410°F).

Lay the tortillas on a baking tray and lightly brush both sides with 2 tablespoons of the olive oil. Season with a pinch of salt and bake in the oven for 6–7 minutes, until crisp and golden. Set aside.

Heat a non-stick frying pan over high heat. Lightly season the kingfish with salt and pepper. Add the remaining olive oil and sear the kingfish for 15 seconds on all sides, then transfer to a plate and set aside.

In a small bowl, mash the avocado with a fork. Add the lemon juice and half the chopped coriander and mix to combine. Season with salt and pepper to taste and set aside.

Slice the tops and bottoms off the blood oranges, then use a small sharp knife to carefully slice the skin away. Carefully cut the segments out and place them in a small bowl, then discard the skin. Add the remaining chopped coriander and a crack of black pepper and gently mix through.

Cut the kingfish into 12 slices. Spoon the mashed avocado onto the tostadas and place two slices of kingfish on each. Top with some of the blood orange, red onion and the whole coriander leaves.

**Green shakshuka,
quinoa and fish**

Pages 70–71

Green shakshuka, quinoa and fish

This nourishing and delicious one-pan dish is an example of how I love to cook at home. It's a great take on classic shakshuka for those who can't eat tomatoes, or want to try a different version.

If you don't have quinoa, use rice. Choose any mix of greens you like or have on hand. If you are catering for multiple dietary needs, bake the fish on a separate tray and keep the shakshuka plant-based.

⅓ cup (80 ml) olive oil

½ small leek, or 1 small brown onion, finely chopped

2 cloves garlic, sliced

Sea salt flakes and ground black pepper

1½ tablespoons *ras el hanout* (see Notes on page 64)

1 small head broccoli, thinly chopped, stalk and all

½ bunch kale or cavolo nero, leaves thinly sliced, stalks discarded

2 zucchinis (courgettes), grated

1 cup (200 g) mixed colour quinoa, rinsed

2½ cups (625 ml) vegetable stock

600 g (1 lb 5 oz) firm white-fleshed fish fillet, such as blue-eye trevalla, gemfish or ling

⅓ cup (80 ml) zhoug or salmoriglio (see page 224, or use a store-bought dairy-free pesto)

1 cup (140 g) frozen peas

Handful coriander (cilantro) leaves, roughly chopped

½ cup (140 g) garlicky whipped tahini (see page 223), or natural Greek-style yoghurt

2 lemons, cut into wedges

Place a large shallow casserole dish or frying pan over medium–high heat. Add 2 tablespoons of the olive oil, the leek or onion, garlic and a pinch of salt. Cook, stirring, for around 3 minutes until the leek is soft, then add the *ras el hanout* and broccoli and continue cooking for 1 minute. Add the kale, zucchini and a crack of pepper and cook for 2 minutes, until the kale begins to wilt.

Add the quinoa to the dish or pan and stir through, then pour in the vegetable stock and stir everything until evenly distributed. Adjust the seasoning and bring to the boil. Cover, reduce the heat to a simmer and cook for 10 minutes.

Season the fish with salt and pepper and gently combine with the remaining olive oil and half the zhoug or salmoriglio. Nestle the fish into the veggies and quinoa, scatter the frozen peas over the top and cover with a lid.

Continue to cook over low heat for a further 10 minutes, keeping an eye on the fish as it cooks; you don't want to overcook it.

Remove the dish or pan from the heat and allow it to stand for 5 minutes. Drizzle with the remaining zhoug or salmoriglio, scatter the coriander over the top and serve with the garlicky whipped tahini or yoghurt and lemon wedges.

Notes I love to make this recipe up to an hour ahead of time and then gently reheat it on the stovetop before serving. Leftovers are also great the next day.

Feel free to try any seasonal fish that's available – this recipe is super versatile, and the gentle cooking method makes it very forgiving.

You could also use basmati rice or freekeh instead of the quinoa, if you like.

Crispy-skin blue-eye with burnt butter, yoghurt, spinach and pine nuts

This is such a delicious dish, which takes some inspiration from *cilbir*, the classic Turkish eggs with yoghurt. Warm, caramelised, lemony butter is so tasty when paired with fish. Blue-eye has a clean, sweet, meaty flavour that's perfect here. If you can't find it, use another firm white-fleshed fish such as ling, snapper, Murray cod or barramundi.

4 x 160 g (5¾ oz) blue-eye trevalla fillets, or any other firm white-fleshed fish fillets, skin on

1 cup (260 g) natural Greek-style yoghurt

1 clove garlic, finely grated

2 lemons, halved

Sea salt flakes and ground black pepper

2 tablespoons olive oil, plus an extra splash

200 g (7 oz) baby spinach leaves

60 g (2¼ oz) unsalted butter

¼ cup (40 g) pine nuts

Pinch of sweet smoked paprika

½ cup (15 g) flat-leaf parsley leaves (optional)

Place the fish fillets on a board, skin-side up. Gently run the back of a knife down the fish's skin to release any moisture, then pat it dry with paper towel. If you have time, let the fish sit in the fridge, uncovered and skin-side up, for at least 2 hours to further dry out.

Combine the yoghurt, garlic, the juice of ½ lemon, some salt and pepper in a bowl. Set aside.

Season both sides of the fish with a little salt. Heat a non-stick frying pan over medium–high heat. Add 2 tablespoons olive oil, then carefully add the fish, skin-side down. Season the flesh with pepper, then firmly press down on the fish with the back of a spatula for 10–20 seconds. Cover with a lid, reduce the heat to medium and cook for a further 3–4 minutes. This allows the flesh to cook gently and the skin to become very crispy. Keep a close eye on the fish, as the cooking time may vary slightly, depending on its thickness.

Turn off the heat, flip the fish over and let it rest in the pan for 1–2 minutes. Transfer to a plate and keep warm.

In a second frying pan, add a splash of olive oil, the spinach, a pinch of salt and a splash of water. Cover with a lid and cook over medium heat until the spinach is wilted, about 30 seconds. Remove the spinach from the heat and drain using a sieve, then transfer to a bowl and set aside.

Discard any oil from the first frying pan and add the butter and pine nuts. Cook over medium heat, stirring, until golden, about 2 minutes. Add the paprika, the juice of ½ lemon and a little salt. Gently combine half of this butter and pine-nut mixture with the spinach.

Spoon the yoghurt onto serving plates. Top with the spinach, a grind of pepper and the fish. Drizzle with the remaining butter and pine-nut mixture. Serve with the parsley (if using) and the remaining lemon juice squeezed over.

Roasted baby carrot and farro salad with carrot-top gremolata

Baby carrots are such a beautiful ingredient and turn any salad into a meal. This dish leaves you feeling so good, thanks to all the nourishing ingredients, and also because you're using the whole carrot, which minimises waste. I love the nutty flavour and chewy texture that farro brings to this salad, but feel free to swap it for any other grains you have on hand.

Preheat the oven to 220°C (425°F) and line a baking tray with baking paper.

Place the farro in a saucepan of boiling water and cook for 15 minutes. Drain, refresh under cold water and transfer to a large bowl. Set aside.

Meanwhile, combine the harissa paste, olive oil and carrots and toss to coat, then season with salt and pepper. Spread the carrots over the tray and roast for 15 minutes, until tender. Reserve any of the left-over roasting oil for the salad.

While the carrots are roasting, make the carrot-top gremolata. Place the chopped carrot tops in a bowl with the capers, garlic and lemon zest. Stir through the lemon juice, olive oil, cumin and chilli flakes (if using). Set aside.

To serve, spoon the green goddess tahini sauce onto a serving tray. Combine the farro, almonds and three-quarters of the gremolata, along with the reserved roasting oil, and toss through. Pile the farro salad over the green goddess tahini sauce and top with the carrots, fennel, avocado and mint. Finish with the remaining gremolata and extra chopped carrot tops.

Pro tip Roast the baby carrots, cook the farro and make the gremolata and green goddess tahini sauce in advance, so you're just tossing it all together to serve.

Note Swap almonds for any other nuts you have on hand, or even toasted pepitas (pumpkin seeds) or sunflower seeds.

1 cup (180 g) farro

1 tablespoon harissa paste

2 tablespoons olive oil

3 bunches baby carrots, washed, trimmed, green tops reserved

Sea salt flakes and ground black pepper

1 cup (265 g) green goddess tahini sauce (see page 222), to serve

½ cup (80 g) almonds (see Note), lightly toasted and crushed

1 small fennel bulb, finely shaved

2 avocados, cut into wedges

Handful mint leaves

Carrot-top gremolata

2 handfuls chopped green carrot tops, plus extra to serve

2 tablespoons capers, drained and chopped

1 clove garlic, crushed

Finely grated zest and juice of 1 lemon

100 ml (3½ fl oz) extra virgin olive oil

1 teaspoon ground cumin

Pinch of dried chilli flakes (optional)

Goes with

· Grilled swordfish skewers
· Pan-fried barramundi fillet
· Grilled Spanish mackerel fillet

Whole roast snapper with red miso butter

This is such a simple yet spectacular dish – a lesson in quality, restraint, and letting a few good ingredients shine. Serve the snapper with something grainy, like rice or quinoa, and a green leafy salad with a sharp dressing. For another vibe, pull the fish off the bone and toss it through some cooked pasta or noodles, using the butter as the decadent sauce.

Don't be limited to just using snapper – try other in-season whole fish like bream, silver perch, flathead or leatherjacket.

2 x 600 g (1 lb 5 oz) whole snappers, cleaned (see Note)

Sea salt flakes and ground black pepper

2 tablespoons olive oil

1 cup (310 g) miso butter (see page 229)

1 bunch chives, finely snipped, to serve

Baby sorrel leaves, to serve (optional)

1 lemon, cut into wedges, to serve

Green leafy salad, to serve

Steamed rice or cooked quinoa, pasta or noodles, to serve

Preheat the oven to 210°C (410°F) and line a large baking tray with baking paper. Remove the fish from the fridge at least 30 minutes in advance, allowing it to come to room temperature and cook evenly.

Dry the fish well with paper towel, then cut three or four shallow slits on both sides and place it on the tray. Season with a little salt and pepper, drizzle with the olive oil and roast in the oven for 10 minutes.

Meanwhile, warm the miso butter in a small saucepan over low heat until it is melted but not split. Spoon a quarter of this over the fish and return it to the oven for a further 5–7 minutes.

Carefully transfer the fish to a serving plate, spoon the remaining miso butter over the top and sprinkle with the chives and baby sorrel leaves, if using. Serve with the lemon wedges, a green leafy salad and the rice, quinoa, pasta or noodles.

Note Ask your fishmonger to clean the fish for you, if you like.

Minestrone verde with poached fish

This is a nourishing soup for those cooler spring days and nights. It features a super-simple poaching technique that is a great way to try different seasonal fish. Pippies or prawns (shrimp) would also work really well, or you could just as easily keep this soup vegetarian by leaving out the seafood and serving it topped with grated parmesan.

⅓ cup (80 ml) olive oil, plus extra to serve

½ leek, washed, halved lengthways and thinly sliced

1 small fennel bulb, sliced, fronds reserved

3 cloves garlic, sliced

Sea salt flakes and ground black pepper

4 zucchinis (courgettes), cut in half lengthways and sliced into 1.5 cm (⅝ inch) rounds

8 cups (2 litres) vegetable or chicken stock

Handful cavolo nero leaves, sliced

1 x 400 g (14 oz) can cannellini (white) beans, rinsed and drained

Handful sugar snap peas or 1 bunch asparagus, sliced on an angle

300 g (10½ oz) firm white-fleshed fish fillet, such as ling, snapper, barramundi or blue-eye trevalla, skin removed and cut into 3 cm (1¼ inch) pieces

1 cup (140 g) frozen peas, thawed

⅓ cup (80 ml) salmoriglio (see page 224)

Finely grated zest and juice of 1 lemon

Pinch of dried chilli flakes (optional)

Heat the olive oil in a large saucepan over medium heat. Add the leek, fennel, garlic and 1 teaspoon salt and cook, stirring often, for 8 minutes. Add the zucchini and cook for a further 5 minutes.

Pour the stock into the pan and bring to the boil, then reduce the heat to low and simmer for 15 minutes. Add the cavolo nero and stir through to wilt the leaves. Adjust the seasoning to taste and add the cannellini beans, sugar snaps or asparagus and fish.

Cover the pan and allow the fish to poach for 3 minutes, then turn the heat off. The fish will continue to cook in the soup.

Lightly crush the peas in a mortar and pestle or in a small food processor. Add the salmoriglio, lemon zest and juice, and season with salt and pepper. Stir to combine.

Ladle the soup into bowls and spoon the pea pesto over the top. Serve with the chilli flakes (if using), the fennel fronds and a splash of extra olive oil.

Fish pho

Pho has to be one of the most nourishing meals around. I love this version with fish and thinly sliced veggies standing in for noodles, as it fills me up without weighing me down. Feel free to swap the veggies for cooked rice noodles, and the fish for prawns (shrimp), if you like – simply poach the prawns in the broth or pan-fry them beforehand.

A vegan version is also delicious – just swap the fish sauce for soy sauce and use an assortment of sautéed mushrooms instead of fish.

300 g (10½ oz) albacore tuna, kingfish or Spanish mackerel

Sea salt flakes and ground black pepper

2 tablespoons olive oil

2 large carrots, peeled

2 large zucchinis (courgettes)

12 snow peas (mange tout), trimmed and thinly sliced

1 cup (115 g) bean sprouts

2 spring onions (scallions), thinly sliced

½ bunch coriander (cilantro), leaves picked

Handful Thai basil leaves

2 limes, halved, to serve

Store-bought chilli sauce, to serve (optional)

Broth

2 tablespoons coriander seeds

3 star anise

2 cinnamon sticks

8 cups (2 litres) chicken, fish or vegetable stock

1 thumb-sized piece ginger, sliced

1 stalk lemongrass, bruised and split

2 tablespoons palm sugar (jaggery)

2 tablespoons fish sauce

To make the broth, place the coriander seeds, star anise and cinnamon sticks in a small frying pan over medium–high heat and toss them continuously for 3 minutes, until toasted. Transfer to a saucepan and add the stock, ginger, lemongrass, palm sugar and fish sauce. Reduce the heat to medium and simmer for 20 minutes, then strain the broth into a separate saucepan and cover with a lid. Let it sit over a low heat to keep it hot.

Meanwhile, place a frying pan over high heat. Season the fish with salt and pepper and drizzle with olive oil. Sear the fish for around 30 seconds each side to caramelise it, then transfer to a plate.

Use a julienne peeler or a mandolin to carefully shred the carrot and zucchini into strips, then divide them among four bowls, along with the snow peas and bean sprouts.

Thinly slice the fish and lay it over the veggies, then scatter the spring onion over the top. Pour the hot broth into each bowl and finish with the coriander and Thai basil leaves and a squeeze of lime juice. Serve with the chilli sauce, if desired.

Pro tip This dish comes together so easily but for an even speedier meal, make the broth and prepare the veggies in advance, and store them in the fridge. Then all that's left to do is sear the fish and reheat the broth to serve.

SUMMER

Grilled haloumi with babaganoush, honey, za'atar and mint

This dish often makes it onto our table, and sits just as perfectly on its own as it does next to some simply cooked seafood. You could also team it with fattoush (page 118).

¼ cup (60 ml) olive oil

250 g (9 oz) haloumi, cut into 5 mm (¼ inch) slices

2 Lebanese cucumbers, cut in half and sliced on an angle

Handful dill sprigs

Handful mint leaves

Handful coriander (cilantro) leaves

1 tablespoon chardonnay vinegar

Sea salt flakes and ground black pepper

2 cups (600 g) babaganoush (see page 229)

2 tablespoons honey

Juice of ½ lemon

1 tablespoon za'atar

Heat a non-stick frying pan over high heat. Add 1 tablespoon of the olive oil and fry the haloumi in batches until caramelised, then transfer to a plate and set aside.

Place the cucumber in a bowl with the herbs, chardonnay vinegar and remaining olive oil and season with salt and pepper. Toss to combine, until the cucumber is well dressed.

To serve, spoon the babaganoush onto serving plates or a large platter and top with the haloumi. Drizzle with the honey and lemon juice, sprinkle with the za'atar and spoon the cucumber salad on top.

Goes with

· Grilled ling skewers
· Whole roasted rainbow trout
· Grilled prawns (shrimp)

Grilled sweet corn and prawns with smoky miso butter

This is carefree summer eating at its best. The charry, nutty grilled corn and sweet prawns (shrimp) are a knockout combination, dialled up with a smoky umami hit of miso and some zesty lime.

1 cup (310 g) miso butter (see page 229), softened

¼ cup (60 g) chipotle in adobo, chopped

12 tiger prawns (shrimp), peeled, deveined, tails intact

2 tablespoons olive oil

4 corn cobs in their husks

Sea salt flakes and ground black pepper

2 spring onions (scallions), green part only, thinly sliced

Pinch of sweet smoked paprika

2 limes, to serve

Soak 12 bamboo skewers in cold water for 10 minutes. Mix the miso butter with the chipotle in a bowl and set aside.

Thread the prawns onto the skewers from their tails through to their heads. Brush with the olive oil and set aside.

Preheat a barbecue or char-grill pan to high.

Peel back the husks of the cobs but don't detach them, then remove and discard the silks (the stringy fibres). Replace the husks and, using a bit of the husk, tie the ends together so the cobs are wrapped once again.

Grill the corn until charred all over, 10–12 minutes, turning them often and brushing a little of the smoky miso butter over them once they begin to colour. Transfer to a plate and cover loosely with foil to keep them warm.

Lightly season the prawns with salt and pepper and grill for 4 minutes, turning them throughout and brushing or spooning a little more smoky miso butter over them when they're nearly done.

To serve, sprinkle the spring onion over the corn, dust with the paprika and squeeze a little lime juice over the top. Serve with the prawns and any remaining smoky miso butter alongside.

Vietnamese summer bowls

I could seriously eat these bowls every day – they're so fresh and vibrant, and the *nuoc cham* dressing is almost good enough to drink. I like to have this on standby in the fridge to dress other salads.

My favourite way to serve this is family-style, by laying out all the components separately so people can help themselves, but you could serve it up individually, too.

16–20 banana prawns (shrimp), peeled and deveined, tails intact

2 tablespoons olive oil

¼ cup (60 ml) smoked chilli and tamarind sauce (see page 228)

Sea salt flakes

150 g (5½ oz) rice vermicelli noodles

2 Lebanese cucumbers, deseeded and cut into matchsticks

2 carrots, peeled and cut into matchsticks

2 handfuls bean sprouts, rinsed and drained

Handful coriander (cilantro) leaves

Handful mint leaves

Nuoc cham dressing

¼ cup (60 ml) fish sauce

¼ cup (60 ml) rice vinegar

Juice of 2 limes

1 tablespoon maple syrup or white sugar

1 clove garlic, finely chopped

1 long red chilli, deseeded (if desired) and finely chopped

Place the prawns, olive oil, smoked chilli and tamarind sauce and a little salt in a bowl and mix to combine. Allow to stand in the fridge for no longer than 1 hour to marinate.

Combine the *nuoc cham* dressing ingredients with ⅓ cup (80 ml) water in a bowl or jar and set aside.

Soak the vermicelli noodles in hot water for 4–5 minutes, then drain and set aside. You don't want to overcook the noodles, so if in doubt, follow the packet instructions.

Place a large char-grill pan or frying pan over medium–high heat. Add the prawns and marinade and cook for around 1 minute each side. Transfer to a plate.

Place the noodles, prawns, matchstick vegetables, sprouts, herbs and *nuoc cham* dressing in individual serving bowls or plates and let everyone build their own summer bowls. If you'd prefer to plate up individually, toss everything together and dress generously with the *nuoc cham* dressing before dividing among bowls and serving.

Note If you haven't made the smoked chilli and tamarind sauce, just season the seafood with a little salt and pepper instead, and add a little olive oil to the pan before grilling the prawns.

Grilled octopus, paprika, potatoes and guindillas

This classic Galician-inspired combo of octopus, paprika and potatoes is popular all over Spain, and epitomises breezy summer eating. Guindillas are green chillies hailing from the Basque region that pack a tangy, spicy punch. This dish goes well with the smoky whole eggplants (page 108) or the 'Big Greek' village salad (page 48).

Sea salt flakes and ground black pepper

2 tablespoons red wine vinegar

1 kg (2 lb 4 oz) cleaned octopus

3 red-skinned potatoes

1 tablespoon sweet smoked paprika

1 clove garlic, crushed

2 tablespoons sherry vinegar

100 ml (3½ fl oz) olive oil

⅓ cup (60 g) green olives

8 guindillas or mild pickled chillies

1 lemon, cut into wedges

Bring a large saucepan of water to the boil. Add 2 teaspoons salt, the red wine vinegar and octopus, using a heatproof plate to keep the octopus submerged. Reduce the heat to a simmer and cook for 35–40 minutes, until the octopus is just tender but the skin is still intact.

Turn the heat off and allow the octopus to rest for 5 minutes, then carefully remove them from the pan. Allow the octopus to cool completely before separating the individual tentacles with a knife, and cutting the heads in half. You can complete up to this point and store the octopus in the fridge for up to 3 days.

Meanwhile, place the potatoes in a saucepan and cover with water. Add 1 teaspoon salt and bring to the boil, then reduce the heat to a simmer and cook for 25–30 minutes, until a skewer or small knife can pierce the potatoes easily, but they're still intact.

Drain the potatoes and allow to cool slightly, then peel them using a small knife and cut into 1 cm (½ inch) thick slices.

Combine the paprika, garlic, sherry vinegar and ⅓ cup (80 ml) of the olive oil in a small bowl and season lightly.

Preheat a barbecue or char-grill pan over high heat. Brush the octopus with the remaining olive oil, season with salt and pepper and grill for 4 minutes, turning a couple of times until lightly charred.

In a bowl, toss the octopus with half the paprika dressing, the green olives and guindillas or chillies.

Place the potatoes on a serving plate and top with the remaining paprika dressing, the octopus, olives, chillies and any remaining octopus juices. Finish with some black pepper and lemon juice squeezed over the top.

Baby cos wedge salad with radish and whipped goat's cheese

This is a simple yet stunning salad to serve up alongside a summer spread. The magic happens in the tangy, creamy dressing that runs through the lettuce veins for fresh, crunchy, next-level deliciousness.

4 baby cos (romaine) lettuces, cut into wedges

Sea salt flakes and ground black pepper

¼ cup (60 ml) extra virgin olive oil

2 tablespoons red wine vinegar

4 radishes, thinly sliced

Handful dill sprigs, roughly chopped

1 lemon, to serve (optional)

Whipped goat's cheese

100 g (3½ oz) soft goat's cheese

⅓ cup (95 g) natural Greek-style yoghurt

2 cloves garlic, crushed

Juice of 1 lemon

To make the whipped goat's cheese, combine all the ingredients with ⅓ cup (80 ml) water in a small blender or food processor and blend until smooth. Set aside.

Place the baby cos, cut-side up, on a large serving plate. Season lightly with salt and pepper and drizzle with the olive oil and vinegar. Spoon the whipped goat's cheese on top and scatter on the radish and dill. Serve with the extra lemon, if you like.

Goes with

· Whole roasted snapper or leatherjacket
· Crumbed ling fillet
· Grilled prawns (shrimp)

Barbecued scallops with ginger, soy and sesame

This is such a delicious mix of flavours. It's a winning dish to make on a warm summer's day as part of a larger spread. The scallops are cooked in their shells, so they're ready in minutes and look amazing. For a more substantial meal, spoon the scallops and dressing over some steamed rice or toss them with cooked soba noodles.

12 scallops in the shell, roe removed

1 vine-ripened tomato, cut into quarters

2 teaspoons toasted sesame seeds

Thinly sliced spring onion (scallion), green part only, to serve

Dressing

2 tablespoons soy sauce

2 tablespoons rice vinegar

2 teaspoons sesame oil

1 teaspoon maple syrup

1 clove garlic, crushed

3 cm (1¼ inch) piece ginger, grated

Preheat a barbecue or char-grill pan to high.

Combine the dressing ingredients in a small bowl and spoon ½ teaspoon over each scallop. Flip the scallops in their shells to coat both sides in the dressing.

Use a sharp knife to remove the seeds from the tomato quarters and discard, then finely dice the flesh. Combine with the remaining dressing and the sesame seeds.

Cook the scallops in their shells for about 1–1½ minutes, then remove them from the heat. Flip the scallops in their shells to warm through the other side. Spoon the tomato dressing over the top, scatter with the spring onion and serve piping hot.

Pan-fried fish with grilled capsicum and olive salad

The big, sweet, meaty flavour of grilled capsicum (pepper) gets me every time. This is the perfect salad to make ahead and dress just before serving. For a larger feast, I suggest serving this with my fattoush (page 118).

500 g (1 lb 2 oz) firm white-fleshed fish fillet, such as blue-eye trevalla, Spanish mackerel or ling, skin on

2 red capsicums (peppers), deseeded and quartered

2 yellow capsicums (peppers), deseeded and quartered

2 small brown onions, cut into 2 cm (¾ inch) wedges

¼ cup (60 ml) olive oil

Sea salt flakes and ground black pepper

½ cup (75 g) pitted kalamata olives

Handful basil leaves

Handful flat-leaf parsley leaves

Handful wild rocket (arugula) leaves

½ cup (80 g) toasted almonds, roughly chopped

Lemony crushed butter beans (see page 230) or babaganoush (see page 229, or use a good-quality store-bought babaganoush), to serve

Dressing

⅓ cup (80 ml) extra virgin olive oil

2 tablespoons sherry vinegar

½ teaspoon ground cumin

½ teaspoon sweet smoked paprika

Place the fish fillets on a board, skin-side up. Gently run the back of a knife down the fish's skin to release any moisture, then pat it dry with paper towel. If you have time, let the fish sit in the fridge, uncovered and skin-side up, for at least 2 hours to further dry out.

Preheat a barbecue or char-grill pan to high.

Toss the capsicum and onion in 2 tablespoons of the olive oil and season with salt and pepper. Grill for 6–8 minutes, turning occasionally, until charred and tender. Transfer to a bowl to cool slightly, then cut or tear in half. Add the olives, half the herbs, the rocket and almonds and mix to combine.

Season both sides of the fish with a little salt. Heat a non-stick frying pan over medium–high heat. Add the remaining oil, then carefully add the fish, skin-side down. Season the flesh with pepper, then firmly press down on the fish with the back of a spatula for 10–20 seconds. Place a lid over the pan, reduce the heat to medium and cook for a further 3–5 minutes. This allows the flesh to cook gently and the skin to become very crispy. Keep a close eye on the fish, as the cooking time may vary slightly, depending on its thickness.

Turn off the heat, flip the fish over and let it rest in the pan for 1–2 minutes. Transfer to a plate and keep warm, then cut into four even portions.

Whisk the dressing ingredients together and season to taste. Pour it over the capsicum salad and toss well to combine.

To serve, spoon some lemony crushed butter beans or babaganoush onto serving plates and top with the capsicum salad, the remaining herbs and the fish.

Avocado love

These avocado recipes are so simple, they'll be on high rotation at your place throughout the warmer months. Serve them as a dip with some raw veggies and crisp pita, or as part of a larger spread alongside other recipes from this book.

Not every avocado is created equal. Delcado Hass avocados, grown in the rich soils of the paradise that is Pemberton, Western Australia, are my avocado of choice when they're in season from September to February. They spend twice as long on the tree as regular avocados, giving them an incredible depth of flavour and a sweet, creamy finish.

Japanese guacamole

Scoop the flesh from 2 avocados into a bowl and mash with a fork. Mix with the juice of ½ lime, 1 tablespoon white miso, 1 teaspoon sesame oil, 2 tablespoons rice vinegar, 2 sliced spring onions (scallions) and a small handful of roughly chopped coriander (cilantro) leaves, and season to taste. Spoon into a serving bowl and top with some blanched edamame, pickled ginger (optional) and toasted white and black sesame seeds. Serve with some nori (dried seaweed) sheets crumbled over the top.

Avocado tzatziki

Scoop the flesh from 2 avocados into a bowl. Mash with a fork and stir through 1 cup (260 g) natural Greek-style yoghurt, 1 grated Lebanese cucumber that has been squeezed dry, 1 clove crushed garlic, 2 tablespoons chardonnay vinegar and a handful of roughly chopped mint leaves. Season with sea salt flakes and ground black pepper, drizzle with extra virgin olive oil and serve topped with thinly sliced radishes, torn extra mint leaves and dill sprigs.

Avocado with peas, watermelon and chilli

Scoop the flesh from 2 avocados and place in a blender with 1 cup (140 g) thawed frozen peas, the juice of 1 lime and some sea salt flakes and ground black pepper. Blend into a rough purée, then spoon into a serving bowl. Cut a small peeled watermelon wedge into 1 cm (½ inch) cubes and scatter over the avocado with some extra thawed frozen peas, a handful of basil leaves, some thinly sliced spring onion (scallion), some sliced green chilli and a crack of black pepper. Finish with an extra squeeze of lime and a splash of extra virgin olive oil.

Romesco tuna toast

This dish brings me nothing but good memories from my time in Spain. It takes me right back to a little wine bar in Madrid, where I would often find myself eating raw fish and romesco toast that had been made using local cod. I couldn't help but order this same dish each time with a glass of Albariño.

This toast is all about the contrast between the warm, smoky charred bread, the sweet, nutty romesco and the delicious meaty tuna. If you prefer your fish cooked, feel free to sear the tuna before slicing it (see page 28).

400 g (14 oz) albacore tuna, cut into 1 cm (½ inch) cubes

Sea salt flakes and ground black pepper

¼ cup (60 ml) olive oil

1–2 tablespoons Calabrian chilli in oil *(see Note on page 60)*, or any chilli in oil

4 large slices sourdough

1 cup (350 g) 3-minute romesco sauce (see page 222)

Small handful basil leaves

Small handful flat-leaf parsley leaves

Small handful dill sprigs

1 lemon, cut into wedges

Place the tuna in a bowl and season lightly with salt and pepper. Dress with 2 tablespoons of the olive oil and the Calabrian chilli and gently mix to combine. Set aside.

Preheat a char-grill pan or barbecue to high, brush the sourdough slices with the remaining olive oil and grill until well charred on both sides.

Spoon the 3-minute romesco sauce over the grilled sourdough, top with the tuna and scatter with the herbs. Serve with the lemon wedges to squeeze over the top.

Barbecued beans with charred spring onion yoghurt

This is a celebration of all the varieties of beans. If you can't get your hands on any of these, swap in asparagus, snow peas (mange tout) or zucchini (courgette) instead. The deep roasty flavour released from the charred spring onion (scallion) makes this dish so spectacular.

300 g (10½ oz) green and yellow beans, trimmed

300 g (10½ oz) butter beans, rinsed and drained

300 g (10½ oz) flat beans, trimmed

4 spring onions (scallions), green part only, cut into 10 cm (4 inch) lengths

2 tablespoons extra virgin olive oil

Sea salt flakes and ground black pepper

1 cup (275 g) sumac yoghurt (see page 223)

2 tablespoons capers, rinsed and drained

⅓ cup (80 g) toasted pepitas (pumpkin seeds)

Large handful wild rocket (arugula) leaves

Handful dill leaves, roughly chopped

Handful mint leaves, roughly chopped

Juice of 1 lemon, to serve

Place the green and yellow beans, butter beans, flat beans, spring onion, olive oil, salt and pepper together in a large bowl and toss to combine.

Preheat a barbecue, char-grill pan or large frying pan to medium and grill the beans and spring onion. Remove the spring onion after 2–3 minutes and leave the beans on for a further minute. You want the spring onion to be charred and soft, and the beans charred but still crunchy. Allow the spring onion to cool, then roughly chop them and combine with the sumac yoghurt. Set aside.

Place the beans in a bowl and allow them to cool to room temperature. Add the capers, pepitas, rocket and half the herbs. Dress with two-thirds of the sumac yoghurt. Toss well and serve with the remaining herbs scattered over the top, the remaining sumac yoghurt drizzled on top and lemon juice squeezed over.

Goes with

· Pan-fried NZ king salmon
· Grilled squid
· Crumbed ling or flathead fillet

Roast tomato and white bean raita

This is part-dip, part-salad, all-out deliciousness that you can eat any time. Pair it with any of the veggie dishes or salads in this book, and some grilled or roasted fish. Use the thickest yoghurt you can find for this recipe.

3 vine-ripened tomatoes, cut in half crossways

¼ cup (60 ml) olive oil

Sea salt flakes and ground black pepper

3 cups (780 g) natural Greek-style yoghurt

1 clove garlic, crushed

¼ cup (40 g) pitted kalamata olives, roughly chopped

Handful coriander (cilantro) leaves, roughly chopped

1 teaspoon brown mustard seeds

1 teaspoon cumin seeds

1 x 400 g (14 oz) can butter beans, rinsed and drained

2 tablespoons zhoug (see page 224), or use a store-bought dairy-free pesto

Handful mint leaves, roughly chopped

Juice of 1 lemon

Extra virgin olive oil, to drizzle

Preheat the oven to 180°C (350°F) and line a baking tray with baking paper.

Place the tomatoes, cut-side up, on the tray, drizzle with 2 tablespoons of the olive oil and lightly season with salt and pepper. Roast for around 40 minutes, until they are soft and wrinkled. Once cooled, roughly chop the tomatoes, reserve a quarter of them and set aside. Combine the remaining tomato with the yoghurt, garlic, olives and coriander.

Place the mustard seeds, cumin seeds and the remaining olive oil in a small frying pan over medium heat and toast the seeds until fragrant. Remove from the heat and add to the yoghurt mixture. Stir to combine, then refrigerate the raita for at least 30 minutes.

Combine the butter beans, zhoug, reserved chopped tomato, mint, lemon juice and a little salt and pepper in a bowl.

To serve, spoon the tomato raita into a serving dish, top with the butter beans and mint and finish with a drizzle of extra virgin olive oil.

Goes with

· Pan-fried red-spot whiting
· Grilled barramundi fillet
· Whole roasted bream

Seared tuna minute steak

This dish is simplicity at its best, taking no longer than 10 minutes from start to finish. It makes the perfect light meal in the warmer months. For a more substantial bowl, toss the seared tuna through some cooked pasta – more on that below!

4 x 150–160 g (5½–5¾ oz) tuna steaks

Sea salt flakes and ground black pepper

⅓ cup (80 ml) olive oil

1 clove garlic, crushed

250 g (9 oz) red grape tomatoes

250 g (9 oz) yellow grape tomatoes

⅓ cup (55 g) pitted kalamata olives, roughly chopped

¼ cup (45 g) capers, rinsed and drained

Handful flat-parsley leaves, roughly chopped

Handful dill sprigs, roughly chopped

1 lemon, cut into wedges, to serve

Extra virgin olive oil, to drizzle

400 g (14 oz) cooked spaghetti, reserving ½ cup (125 ml) starchy pasta cooking water (optional)

Dried chilli flakes (optional)

Preheat a large non-stick frying pan, char-grill pan or barbecue over high heat.

Season the tuna steaks with salt and pepper and drizzle with 2 tablespoons of the olive oil. Cook in batches for 30 seconds on one side and remove from the pan without flipping. If you prefer your tuna well done, cook for 30 seconds each side and then transfer to a plate to rest for 1–2 minutes.

Add the remaining olive oil to the pan with the garlic, tomatoes and a pinch of salt. Cook until the tomatoes begin to burst, then add the olives, capers and a crack of pepper. Add the herbs and stir through.

To serve the tuna as it is (pictured opposite), spoon the tomatoes over it. Squeeze the lemon juice over the top and finish with a drizzle of extra virgin olive oil.

To serve the tuna with pasta, slice it into thin strips and combine with the cooked spaghetti, tomato and herb sauce, reserved starchy pasta cooking water and a good glug of extra virgin olive oil. Finish with a squeeze of lemon juice and dried chilli flakes, if you like.

Smoky whole eggplants with crispy chickpeas, olives and tahini

No other vegetable gets me more excited than charred eggplant – it's a feast for the senses and takes me straight back to my childhood. Cooking vegetables whole this way is so often overlooked, but it's a great technique for coaxing amazing flavour out of ingredients without fuss. This recipe also forms the base for babaganoush – see page 229 for that recipe.

5 eggplants (aubergines)

Sea salt flakes and ground black pepper

2 tablespoons extra virgin olive oil

2 tablespoons chilli oil

Juice of 1 lemon

2 tablespoons pomegranate molasses

To serve

⅔ cup (185 g) garlicky whipped tahini (see page 223)

2 tablespoons za'atar

⅓ cup (55 g) pitted kalamata olives, roughly chopped

1 cup (175 g) crispy roast chickpeas (see page 230)

Handful dill sprigs, roughly chopped

Handful mint leaves, roughly chopped

Preheat a barbecue to high and cook the eggplants whole for 15 minutes, turning throughout, until the skins are charred and the eggplants are soft. Alternatively, working in batches, place the whole eggplants over an open gas cooker flame and cook for 10 minutes, turning throughout, until soft. You can also bake them by placing them directly onto the oven racks and cooking at 230°C (450°F) for 20–25 minutes, until soft (though you won't get the same smoky flavour).

Place the cooked eggplants on a wire rack set over a plate or tray and allow them to drain and cool for a few minutes, then carefully peel off the burnt skin, leaving the eggplants whole and the tops intact, if possible. Carefully transfer them to a serving platter, season with salt and pepper, then drizzle with the olive oil, chilli oil, lemon juice and pomegranate molasses.

To serve, spoon the garlicky whipped tahini over the eggplants and sprinkle with the za'atar. Top with the olives, crispy roast chickpeas and herbs, and dig in.

Goes with

· Seared tuna or kingfish fillet
· Grilled NZ king salmon fillet
· Grilled ling fillet

Rainbow trout with peach, sweet potato and charred onion salad

This satisfying salad is summer goodness at its best. Charred onion is a great way to add flavour to salads and teams so well with the sweet peaches. Some marinated feta or torn fresh mozzarella is also a welcome addition.

3 sweet potatoes (kumara), cut in half lengthways

2 red onions, peeled and cut into six wedges each

⅓ cup (80 ml) olive oil

Sea salt flakes and ground black pepper

4 peaches, cut into wedges

2 baby cos (romaine) lettuces, inner leaves only

1 fennel bulb, finely shaved

3 spring onions (scallions), sliced

Handful basil leaves

1 cup (140 g) walnuts, toasted and roughly chopped

1 x whole rainbow trout, cleaned (see Note on page 76), weighing approximately 500–600 g (1 lb 2 oz–1 lb 5 oz)

1 lemon, halved

2 tablespoons chardonnay vinegar

⅓ cup (80 ml) extra virgin olive oil

100 g (3½ oz) marinated feta or fresh mozzarella, torn, to serve (optional)

Preheat the oven to 200°C (400°F) and line a baking tray with baking paper.

In a bowl, toss the sweet potato, red onion, 2 tablespoons of the olive oil and some salt and pepper together. Place on the tray and roast for around 25–30 minutes, until the sweet potato is cooked and the onion is soft and charred. Allow to cool, then tear the sweet potato into large pieces and transfer to a bowl with the red onion, peaches, baby cos, fennel, spring onion, basil and walnuts.

Place the rainbow trout on a baking tray lined with baking paper and make three shallow cuts down both sides of the fish. Lightly season with salt and pepper and drizzle with the remaining olive oil. Cut a lemon half into three slices and insert these inside the fish belly's cavity. Roast for around 12 minutes, then let it rest for 4 minutes.

Drizzle the salad with the chardonnay vinegar and extra virgin olive oil, then season with a little salt and pepper and gently toss to combine. Flake the rainbow trout over it, top with the feta or torn mozzarella (if using) and serve with the juice from the remaining lemon half squeezed over.

Summer Fish Tacos
Pages 114–115

Summer fish tacos

This recipe is all about inviting family or friends over and getting stuck into an easy meal together. For a lighter vibe, replace the tortillas with large lettuce cups.

Baking fish is such an easy and mess-free way to cook it, and these tacos are a delicious vehicle for trying different species. I have suggested fillets, but a couple of 700 g (1 lb 9 oz) whole fish would also work, as would prawns (shrimp); you just need to adjust the cooking time – about 15–20 minutes for fish, and 4 minutes for peeled banana or tiger prawns.

800 g (1 lb 12 oz) firm white-fleshed fish fillet, such as ling, flathead, gurnard or barramundi

Sea salt flakes and ground black pepper

½ cup (125 ml) Everything Mexican marinade and dressing (see page 225)

2 corn cobs, husks removed

2 tablespoons olive oil

1 small red onion, finely chopped

1 bunch coriander (cilantro), leaves picked and roughly chopped

2 vine-ripened tomatoes, diced

4 limes, plus lime wedges, to serve

16 small corn tortillas

2 avocados, sliced

Pickled jalapeños, to serve

Yoghurt sauce

1 cup (260 g) natural Greek-style yoghurt

1 clove garlic, crushed

Finely grated zest and juice of 1 lime

Pinch of sweet smoked paprika

Place the fish in a baking dish, season lightly with salt and pour the Everything Mexican marinade and dressing over the top. Allow to stand in the fridge for 30 minutes to marinate, if you can.

Preheat a barbecue or char-grill pan to high. Rub the corn with half the olive oil and grill, turning often, for 10 minutes, until charred. Allow to cool, then carefully slice the kernels off the cobs and place in a bowl with half the red onion and half the coriander.

Place the tomato in a second bowl with the remaining red onion and coriander. Squeeze the limes over both the corn mixture and the tomato mixture, season each with salt and pepper and drizzle the remaining olive oil over each. Mix each bowl thoroughly and set aside.

To make the yoghurt sauce, combine all the ingredients in a bowl, season to taste and set aside.

Preheat the oven to 200°C (400°F). Place the fish and all its marinade on a baking tray lined with baking paper and bake for 8–10 minutes, until it just starts to flake away with light pressure from a fork at its thickest part.

While the fish is cooking, warm the tortillas over the hot grill for 10 seconds each side. Wrap them in a clean tea towel to keep warm.

Place the sliced avocado on a plate. Transfer the fish and any remaining marinade to a separate plate and serve with the corn, tomato salsa and jalapeños, letting everyone build their own tacos. The idea is to fill a warm tortilla with a little corn, avocado, some salsa, fish and jalapeños, then finish with a drizzle of the yoghurt sauce and a squeeze of lime juice.

Pro tip To make serving time a breeze, prep everything in advance up until cooking the fish and warming the tortillas. You could also marinate the fish up to 3 hours in advance and leave it in the fridge, then take it out 30 minutes before cooking to bring it to room temperature.

Whole roast Lebanese fish

This marinade is so delicious, inspired by the classic za'atar roast chicken. It makes for an impressive yet simple dinner. Turn this into a feast by serving it with fattoush (page 118), sumac yoghurt (page 223) and flatbread. I love leatherjacket – it's such a delicious, sustainable choice – but you could also use rainbow trout, barramundi, bream or snapper.

Please don't shy away from cooking whole fish – it's easy, mess-free and tastes amazing. If you're still not convinced, you could use a large white-fleshed fish fillet for this recipe, which takes even less time to cook (around 8–10 minutes).

3 x 400–500 g (14 oz–1 lb 2 oz) whole leatherjackets, cleaned, or 2 x 750 g (1 lb 10 oz) whole rainbow trout, barramundi, bream or snapper, cleaned (see Note on page 76)

Sea salt flakes and ground black pepper

⅓ cup (50 g) pine nuts, toasted

Handful flat-leaf parsley leaves

½ small red onion, thinly sliced

Flatbread or steamed rice, to serve

Marinade

¼ cup (60 ml) olive oil

Juice of 1 lemon, plus ½ lemon extra, sliced

2 tablespoons honey

2 tablespoons za'atar, plus extra to serve

1 teaspoon sweet smoked paprika, plus extra to serve

2 teaspoons sumac

1 teaspoon ground cinnamon

½ teaspoon mixed spice

4 cloves garlic, roughly chopped

Pat each fish inside and out with paper towel until dry, then make three shallow cuts down both sides of each fish. Place in a wide shallow bowl or a deep baking dish and season with salt and pepper.

In a small bowl, combine the marinade ingredients, then pour over each fish and into the cavities, making sure the fish is very well coated. Allow to stand in the fridge for at least 1 hour to marinate, then remove from the fridge 30 minutes before cooking to let the fish come to room temperature and cook more evenly.

Preheat the oven to 220°C (425°F).

Place the fish and all the marinade in a large baking tray lined with baking paper and roast for 15–20 minutes, then allow it to rest for 2–3 minutes.

Sprinkle a little extra paprika and za'atar over the fish. Combine the pine nuts, parsley and red onion and scatter over the top. Serve with some flatbread or steamed rice.

Fattoush

Fattoush and tabouli were the main two salads I grew up eating, and they were everything to me. Both were made using what was growing in our garden or between the cracks in our footpath, which was usually purslane, an edible weed.

I love fattoush, because I usually have all the ingredients in the fridge and some Lebanese bread in the freezer. It's so adaptable with whatever you have on hand and comes together so quickly. Please don't feel limited by this recipe – if you have capsicum (pepper), red cabbage, carrot or even avocado, you can use them. Think outside the box – add some roast eggplant (aubergine), or in winter try roast cauliflower and kale instead of tomatoes and cucumbers. It's not traditional, but that's not a reason not to enjoy something. Make it wild and delicious!

2 pieces Lebanese flatbread, cut into quarters

1 tablespoon olive oil

3 handfuls fresh herbs, such as mint, flat-leaf parsley or dill, roughly chopped

4 radishes, cut into wedges, green tops reserved and roughly chopped

3 Lebanese cucumbers, cut into wedges

4 vine-ripened tomatoes, cut into wedges

2 spring onions (scallions), green part only, thinly sliced

2 small gem lettuces

Sea salt flakes and ground black pepper

Sumac dressing

1 tablespoon sumac

1 tablespoon pomegranate molasses

⅓ cup (80 ml) olive oil

Juice of 1 lemon

Preheat the oven to 180°C (350°F).

Brush the bread with the olive oil, place on a baking tray and bake for 5 minutes, until crisp. Set aside.

In a large bowl, combine the herbs, radish, radish tops, cucumber, tomato and spring onion. Set aside.

Roughly chop the larger outer lettuce leaves. Cut the small inner hearts in half lengthways and place both in a serving dish or bowl.

To make the sumac dressing, whisk all the ingredients together.

Pour half of the dressing over the radish salad and the other half over the lettuce. Season both with salt and pepper, then add the crisp bread to the radish salad and toss gently.

To serve, scatter the radish salad over the lettuce.

Pro tip To create a feast, serve this with my whole roast Lebanese fish (page 116), some babaganoush (page 229), hummus (see page 38) and garlicky whipped tahini (page 223).

Note For a tasty gluten-free version, swap the bread for 1 cup (175 g) of my crispy roast chickpeas (page 230).

Goes with

· Whole roasted leatherjacket or bream
· Grilled ling skewers
· Grilled prawns (shrimp)

Summer seafood pasta

This seafood pasta is for when you want to add a little luxe to your week. It's a flex, showcasing some amazing seafood. What makes this dish stand out for me is the way the pasta is cooked in white wine and shellfish juices, similar to the absorption method used to make risotto – it creates so much flavour with such little effort. I was making one-pot pasta dishes this way when I was a young apprentice living in a small apartment, long before I ever formally learned this technique.

⅓ cup (80 ml) extra virgin olive oil, plus extra to drizzle

2 red (Asian) shallots, thinly sliced

3 cloves garlic, sliced

1 teaspoon dried chilli flakes

Sea salt flakes

300 ml (10½ fl oz) white wine

500 g (1 lb 2 oz) pippies, scrubbed

500 g (1 lb 2 oz) mussels, scrubbed and debearded

1¼ cups (310 ml) fish stock

500 g (1 lb 2 oz) dried linguine

16 banana prawns (shrimp), peeled, deveined and cut in half lengthways, tails intact (optional)

250 g (9 oz) grape tomatoes, cut in half

Large handful flat-leaf parsley leaves, roughly chopped

Juice of 1 lemon

Place a large, deep frying pan (big enough to hold all the seafood and pasta) over medium–high heat. Add the olive oil, shallot, garlic, chilli flakes and a pinch of salt. Cook, stirring, for 3 minutes until the shallot is soft and very fragrant, then add the white wine, pippies and mussels. Cover with a lid and cook for 2–3 minutes, allowing them to steam until they open. Using tongs or a slotted spoon, transfer the pippies and mussels to a bowl once open.

Add the fish stock and around 1¼ cups (310 ml) water to the pan and bring to the boil, then add the pasta and stir immediately for 1 minute to prevent it from sticking together. Continue to cook, stirring often, for 5 minutes and adding more water as needed, to allow the pasta to cook evenly. Add the prawns and tomatoes, stir through and cook for a further 3 minutes. Continue adding a little water to the pasta as needed, to create a nice loose sauce.

Return the pippies and mussels to the pan with any juices, then add the parsley and lemon juice and toss through. Adjust the seasoning to taste and serve immediately with a drizzle of extra olive oil.

Pro tip Prepare everything before you begin cooking, so you're always in control, and not panicked or rushed.

Crispy-skin barramundi with nectarine, chilli and herb salad

Make the most of in-season nectarines with this delicious, simple, toss-and-dress salad, a perfect match for the crispy-skin barra. The sweet stonefruit works so well with the other savoury, spicy flavours.

4 x 180 g (6⅓ oz) barramundi fillets, or other fish such as NZ king salmon, snapper or mulloway, skin on

3 ripe yellow nectarines, cut into wedges

3 ripe white nectarines, cut into wedges

2 avocados, cut into thick wedges

1 long red chilli, deseeded and thinly sliced

Handful coriander (cilantro) leaves, roughly chopped

Handful mint leaves, roughly chopped

2 spring onions (scallions), thinly sliced

Handful baby spinach leaves

1 tablespoon sesame oil

⅓ cup (80 ml) olive oil

2 tablespoons rice vinegar

Juice of 1 lime

½ cup (70 g) roasted peanuts, roughly chopped

Sea salt flakes and ground black pepper

Place the fish fillets on a board, skin-side up. Gently run the back of a knife down the fish's skin to release any moisture, then pat it dry with paper towel. If you have time, let the fish sit in the fridge, uncovered and skin-side up, for at least 2 hours to further dry out.

In a large bowl, combine the yellow and white nectarines with the avocado, chilli, herbs, spring onion and spinach leaves. Drizzle with the sesame oil and 2 tablespoons of the olive oil, followed by the rice vinegar and lime juice. Toss gently to coat, then sprinkle with the peanuts.

Season both sides of the fish with a little salt. Heat a non-stick frying pan over medium–high heat. Add the remaining olive oil, then carefully add the fish, skin-side down. Season the flesh with pepper, then firmly press down on the fish with the back of a spatula for 10–20 seconds. Place a lid over the pan, reduce the heat to medium and cook for a further 3–5 minutes. This allows the flesh to cook gently and the skin to become very crispy. Keep a close eye on the fish, as the cooking time may vary slightly, depending on its thickness.

Turn off the heat, flip the fish over and let it rest in the pan for 1–2 minutes. Transfer to a plate and keep warm.

Serve the crispy-skin fish with the nectarine salad.

Grilled split prawns and squid with zhoug

Nothing screams summer like a plate of grilled prawns (shrimp). The spicy zhoug works a treat against the sweetness of the seafood, with the sumac yoghurt offering some cool respite. Create a feast by pairing it with other dishes such as hummus (page 38), babaganoush (page 229) and fattoush (page 118).

12 large tiger prawns (shrimp), shells on

4 squid, cleaned and dried with paper towel

Sea salt flakes and ground black pepper

⅓ cup (80 ml) zhoug (see page 224)

2 tablespoons olive oil

Sumac yoghurt (see page 223), to serve (optional)

2 lemons, cut into wedges, to serve

To butterfly the prawns, lay them flat on their side and use the tip of a sharp knife to make an incision from head to tail, through the belly side, being careful not to cut all the way to the back. Use the tip of your knife to carefully remove the vein.

To score the squid, cut the squid tubes open and, using the tip of a sharp knife, make shallow criss-cross incisions to create diamond patterns.

Place the butterflied prawns in a shallow bowl and place the squid in a separate bowl. Season both with salt and pepper and divide the zhoug and olive oil between each, tossing gently to coat. Cover and place both bowls in the fridge for 30–60 minutes to marinate.

Preheat a barbecue or char-grill pan to high and grill the prawns, shell-side down, for 2 minutes, then flip and cook for 20 seconds. Remove from the heat and allow to rest while you cook the squid.

Cook the squid, scored-side down, for 4 minutes, turning halfway, until curled and charred. Allow to rest for 1 minute.

Serve the prawns and squid with some sumac yoghurt and the lemon wedges.

Pro tip Prepare and marinate the prawns up to 2 hours in advance. I suggest splitting and grilling the prawns in their shells, which protects them during cooking, but you could easily peel and devein them if you prefer, and leave their heads and tails intact for great presentation.

Note You could also slice the cooked squid thickly before serving, if you prefer.

Crumbed fish Niçoise

This is by far the most versatile salad, in terms of what you can pair with it. I love the contrast between the crumbed fish and the cool, fresh, crunchy veggies.

Flathead is such a delicious fish here in Australia, but I have listed some great substitutes below if you can't find it. If you want an even lighter version, use grilled or pan-fried fish, prawns (shrimp) or squid.

½ cup (70 g) plain (all-purpose) flour

Sea salt flakes and ground black pepper

½ teaspoon garlic powder (optional)

½ teaspoon onion powder (optional)

600 g (1 lb 5 oz) skinless, boneless flathead fillet, or any other firm white-fleshed fish, such as ling, whiting or bream, cut into 8 cm x 2 cm (3¼ x ¾ inch) pieces

2 free-range eggs, lightly whisked, plus 4 eggs extra

1½ cups (90 g) panko breadcrumbs

400 g (14 oz) green beans, trimmed

Iced water

8 kipfler (fingerling) or new chat potatoes, scrubbed

⅓ cup (80 ml) olive oil

2 tablespoons red wine vinegar

⅓ cup (80 ml) extra virgin olive oil

1 butter lettuce or baby cos (romaine) lettuce

500 g (1 lb 2 oz) grape or cherry tomatoes, cut in half

6 small radishes, quartered

½ cup (95 g) kalamata olives

2 tablespoons baby capers, rinsed and drained

Handful basil leaves

1 lemon, cut into wedges

Combine the flour, a little salt and pepper, and the garlic and onion powders (if using) in a bowl. Toss the fish in the flour mixture, shaking off any excess, then dip in the whisked eggs, draining any excess. Roll the fish in the panko, pressing the crumbs into each piece to coat well. Place on a baking tray and refrigerate for at least 5 minutes.

Bring a large saucepan of water to the boil, lightly season it with salt and add the green beans. Cook the beans for 1½ minutes, then use tongs or a slotted spoon to transfer them to a bowl of iced water to refresh for 1 minute. Drain well on crumpled paper towel and set aside.

Add the extra four eggs to the boiling water and cook for 6 minutes, then transfer to the iced water to refresh for 2 minutes. Drain the eggs, then carefully peel and cut them in half. Set aside.

Add the potatoes to the boiling water and cook until tender, around 12 minutes. Drain and slice into rounds.

Heat the olive oil in a frying pan over medium–high heat. Cook the fish in batches for 2–3 minutes each side, until golden and cooked through. Drain on paper towel. Alternatively, bake the fish on a lightly greased wire rack placed over a baking tray in an oven preheated to 220°C (425°F) for 8 minutes.

While the fish is cooking, combine the red wine vinegar, extra virgin olive oil and a little salt and pepper in a small bowl. Separate the lettuce leaves and place them on a serving tray. Spoon a little of the dressing over the top, then scatter the potatoes, tomatoes, green beans, radish, olives, capers and basil over the lettuce. Finish with the eggs and spoon the remaining dressing over everything. Serve the salad with the crumbed fish and the lemon wedges.

AUTUMN

Crispy brussels sprouts with tahini, maple, chilli, za'atar and mint

Brussels sprouts are definitely having their time in the sun. They also happen to be one of my all-time favourite vegetables, especially when they're roasted like this, which caramelises them and turns them all gnarly. I could eat this whole dish myself (and often do) but you could also pair it with so many other dishes from the Autumn and Winter chapters.

¼ cup (60 ml) olive oil

500 g (1 lb 2 oz) small brussels sprouts, cut in half

Sea salt flakes

1 cup (375 g) crispy roast chickpeas (see page 230)

½ long red chilli, deseeded and finely chopped

2 tablespoons maple syrup

Juice of 1 lemon

1 cup (280 g) garlicky whipped tahini (see page 223)

Handful mint leaves

2 tablespoons za'atar

Preheat the oven to 210°C (410°F).

Place an ovenproof frying pan over high heat and add the olive oil, brussels sprouts and a good pinch of salt. Fry the sprouts, tossing regularly, until they begin to colour, then transfer the pan to the oven and roast for a further 10 minutes, until they are caramelised.

Remove the brussels sprouts from the oven and add half the crispy roast chickpeas, the chilli, maple syrup and lemon juice and toss through. Top with the remaining crispy roast chickpeas, garlicky whipped tahini, mint leaves and za'atar, and serve.

Goes with

· Pan-fried gemfish fillet
· Grilled NZ king salmon fillet
· Roasted ling fillet

Crispy-skin fish with barbecued eggplant, lemony lentils and yoghurt

This is my go-to technique for producing a crispy fish skin every time. It's served here with smoky, fall-apart eggplant (aubergine) and zesty, herby lentils, before being blanketed in a garlicky yoghurt for next-level yum.

4 x 160 g (5¾ oz) bream fillets, or any other firm-fleshed fish, such as snapper, barramundi or kingfish

1 eggplant (aubergine), cut into 1 cm (½ inch) thick rounds

100 ml (3½ fl oz) olive oil, plus 2 tablespoons extra, for brushing

Sea salt flakes and ground black pepper

1 x 400 g (14 oz) can lentils, rinsed and drained

Handful pitted kalamata olives, roughly chopped

100 g (3½ oz) grape tomatoes, cut in half

2 handfuls mixed herbs, such as flat-leaf parsley, basil or dill, leaves picked

2 spring onions (scallions), thinly sliced

Finely grated zest and juice of 1 lemon

1 clove garlic, crushed (optional)

½ teaspoon sweet smoked paprika

2 tablespoons sherry vinegar

1 cup (275 g) sumac yoghurt (see page 223)

Place the fish fillets on a board, skin-side up. Gently run the back of a knife down the fish's skin to release any moisture, then pat it dry with paper towel. If you have time, let the fish sit in the fridge, uncovered and skin-side up, for at least 2 hours to further dry out.

Preheat a barbecue or char-grill pan to high. Brush the eggplant with 2 tablespoons of the olive oil, then season with salt and pepper. Cook for 4 minutes, turning halfway, until it's nice and charred, then transfer to a plate and allow it to cool slightly.

In a large bowl, combine the eggplant, lentils, olives, tomatoes, herbs and spring onion. Dress with the lemon zest and juice, the garlic (if using), paprika, vinegar and ⅓ cup (80 ml) of the olive oil. Season to taste with salt and pepper and toss to combine.

Season both sides of the fish with a little salt. Heat a non-stick frying pan over medium–high heat. Add the remaining olive oil, then carefully add the fish, skin-side down. Season the flesh with pepper, then firmly press down on the fish with the back of a spatula for 10–20 seconds. Cover with a lid, reduce the heat to medium and cook for a further 3–4 minutes. This allows the flesh to cook gently and the skin to become very crispy. Keep a close eye on the fish, as the cooking time may vary slightly, depending on its thickness.

Turn off the heat, flip the fish over and let it rest in the pan for 1–2 minutes. Transfer to a plate and keep warm.

Serve the fish with the eggplant salad and the sumac yoghurt spooned over the top.

Tray-roasted almost ratatouille

The further you delve into cultures and their food history, the more you realise how certain flavour and ingredient combinations are prevalent across the globe. Take eggplant (aubergine), tomatoes, zucchini (courgette) and capsicum (pepper), for example; this mix is just as much Middle Eastern as it is Mediterranean. Keep this dish plant-based by leaving out the fish and serving it with the salmoriglio, and some feta or yoghurt.

1 large eggplant (aubergine), cut into 3 cm (1¼ inch) pieces

3 zucchinis (courgettes), cut into 3 cm (1¼ inch) rounds

1 large red capsicum (pepper), cut into 3 cm (1¼ inch) lengths

1 red onion, peeled and cut into 1.5 cm (⅝ inch) pieces

1 large red-skinned potato, such as desiree, cut into 3 cm (1¼ inch) pieces

⅓ cup (80 ml) olive oil, plus extra to drizzle

3 cloves garlic, smashed

Sea salt flakes and ground black pepper

500 g (1 lb 2 oz) ling fillet, or any other firm white-fleshed fish, such as blue-eye trevalla, barramundi, gemfish or snapper

⅓ cup (80 ml) salmoriglio (see recipe, page 224)

1 x 400 g (14 oz) can cherry tomatoes

Handful flat-leaf parsley leaves

1 lemon, cut into wedges

Preheat the oven to 220°C (425°F) and line a baking tray with baking paper.

Combine the eggplant, zucchini, capsicum, onion, potato, olive oil, garlic, salt and plenty of black pepper in a bowl and toss well. Scatter on the tray, cover with foil and roast for 45 minutes.

Meanwhile, place the fish on a plate, coat it in the salmoriglio and a little salt and pepper and let it marinate for up to 30 minutes in the fridge. Bring it out of the fridge 30 minutes before cooking to bring it to room temperature.

Remove the foil from the tray, add the tomatoes and stir, then nestle the fish in the veggies. Roast, uncovered, for a further 10 minutes, until the fish is just cooked and the tomatoes burst open.

Scatter the parsley over the fish and serve with the lemon wedges and a drizzle of olive oil.

Marinated beetroots, whipped feta, lentils and za'atar

I love the combo of sweet, earthy beetroots and tangy, salty feta together. This salad works as a stand-alone dish or pairs amazingly with fish, hummus or my whipped pumpkin tahini (page 152). Lentils can easily be switched with farro, freekeh, buckwheat or quinoa. Feel free to swap the feta for sumac yoghurt (page 223).

4–5 beetroots

⅓ cup (80 ml) red wine vinegar, plus 2 tablespoons extra

2 tablespoons caster (superfine) sugar

2 tablespoons sea salt flakes

1 x 400 g (14 oz) can lentils, rinsed and drained

1 small fennel bulb, finely shaved, fronds reserved

Handful wild rocket (arugula) leaves

⅓ cup (45 g) slivered almonds, toasted

Handful mint leaves

Handful dill sprigs

1 teaspoon za'atar, plus extra to serve

⅓ cup (80 ml) extra virgin olive oil

1 tablespoon pomegranate molasses

Whipped feta

150 g (5½ oz) soft feta, such as Danish feta, crumbled

⅓ cup (95 g) natural Greek-style yoghurt

Juice of ½ lemon

1 tablespoon olive oil

Ground black pepper, to taste

Place the beetroots in a large saucepan and fill with enough water to cover them. Add the vinegar, sugar and salt and bring to the boil. Reduce the heat to a simmer and cook for 1 hour or until soft. You want to be able to pierce through the beetroot easily with a small knife or skewer.

Meanwhile, make the whipped feta by placing all the ingredients in a small food processor or blender with 2 tablespoons water and blending until smooth, light and fluffy. You might need to add a little more water, depending on the feta. Season to taste with more lemon juice, salt or pepper, if desired.

Peel the beetroots while they're still warm, then cut into wedges and place in a bowl. Add the lentils, fennel, rocket, almonds and herbs.

Whisk together the extra 2 tablespoons of the vinegar, the za'atar, olive oil and pomegranate molasses and season with salt and pepper. Pour this dressing over the salad and toss to combine.

Smear some whipped feta generously over a serving plate and pile the salad on top. Finish with a little more za'atar and serve.

Pro tip Cook the beetroots ahead of time, as they last up to 4 days in the fridge. Whipped feta can harden in the fridge, so if you make it in advance, bring it out of the fridge 15 minutes before serving and give it a good whip with a spoon.

Goes with

· Whole roasted rainbow trout
· Pan-fried ocean trout fillet
· Pan-fried blue-eye trevalla fillet

Mexican sweet potatoes

This is a delicious 'meaty' vegetarian dish, finished with some natural yoghurt, which works so well with all the warm toasty spices. It's definitely brawny enough to stand on its own, but is just as at home next to your favourite fish or seafood dishes.

4 sweet potatoes (kumara)

2 tablespoons olive oil

2 cups (180 g) button mushrooms, finely chopped

1 small brown onion, finely chopped

2 cloves garlic, finely chopped

Sea salt flakes

2 teaspoons ground cumin

1 teaspoon sweet smoked paprika

Pinch of dried chilli flakes (optional)

2 tablespoons tomato paste (concentrated purée)

1 x 400 g (14 oz) can black beans, rinsed and drained

200 ml (7 fl oz) vegetable stock

1 cup (260 g) natural Greek-style yoghurt

2 tablespoons store-bought chilli sauce (optional)

1 large avocado, cut into wedges

Handful coriander (cilantro) leaves

2 limes, cut in half

Preheat the oven to 190°C (375°F).

Place the sweet potatoes on a baking tray lined with baking paper. Prick them a couple of times with a fork, cover with foil and roast for around 45 minutes, until soft.

Meanwhile, heat a saucepan over medium–high heat and add the olive oil, mushrooms, onion, garlic and a pinch of salt. Cook, stirring, for 5 minutes, until the mushrooms and onion have softened and everything smells amazing.

Add the spices, dried chilli (if using), tomato paste and black beans to the pan and cook for 2 more minutes, then add the vegetable stock and cook until the mixture has thickened, 5–10 minutes. Adjust the seasoning to taste and set aside.

Swirl together the yoghurt and chilli sauce (if using) in a bowl. Cut the sweet potatoes in half and lightly season the flesh with salt. Spoon the mushrooms over them, followed by the chilli yoghurt and avocado. Scatter the coriander over the top and serve with a squeeze of lime juice.

Goes with

· Grilled tiger prawns (shrimp)
· Grilled kingfish fillet
· Pan-fried snapper fillet

Mandarin, avocado and soba noodle salad

This dish is for when you want something fresh, zingy and super easy. Sweet and subtly tart mandarins work so well in this light Asian-inspired dressing. I love this salad as it is or served alongside some kingfish sashimi. You could also try pan-fried prawns (shrimp) or flaked ocean trout tossed through it.

200 g (7 oz) dried buckwheat soba noodles

2 spring onions (scallions), thinly sliced

2 yellow capsicums (peppers), thinly sliced

2 avocados, sliced

4 mandarins, peeled and cut into pieces

1 long green chilli, deseeded and finely sliced (optional)

Handful coriander (cilantro) leaves

Sea salt flakes

½ cup (80 g) cashew nuts, toasted and roughly chopped

Sesame soy dressing

¼ cup (60 ml) rice wine vinegar

2 tablespoons sesame oil

2 tablespoons soy sauce or tamari

1 tablespoon black sesame seeds, toasted

To make the sesame soy dressing, combine the vinegar, sesame oil, soy sauce or tamari and half the sesame seeds in a small bowl and whisk to combine. Set aside.

Bring a saucepan of water to the boil and cook the soba noodles for 4 minutes. Refresh under cold water, then drain well and mix with ¼ cup (60 ml) of the dressing and half the spring onion. Divide between four serving bowls.

Combine the capsicum, avocado, mandarin and chilli (if using) in a large bowl with the remaining spring onion, half the coriander, a little salt and some of the dressing. Gently toss to combine, then divide between the noodle bowls.

Spoon any remaining dressing over the top, then scatter with the cashew nuts and the remaining coriander and black sesame seeds.

Goes with

· Seared kingfish or tuna sashimi
· Poached ocean trout fillet
· Pan-fried tiger prawns (shrimp)

Crispy-skin Spanish mackerel with roast grape, olive and almond salad

This is a stunning dish. Roasting the grapes intensifies their flavour, which works so perfectly with the fish. Roast some extra grapes and store them in the fridge for a few days – they're great in salads or on charred bread with ricotta. Turn this into a more substantial meal by serving some couscous or a herby grain salad alongside.

4 x 185 g (6½ oz) Spanish mackerel fillets, skin on

250 g (9 oz) red seedless grapes

½ cup (125 ml) olive oil, plus 1 tablespoon extra

Sea salt flakes and ground black pepper

⅓ cup (55 g) pitted kalamata olives, roughly chopped

⅓ cup (45 g) slivered almonds, toasted

1 small celery stick, thinly sliced

Handful flat-leaf parsley leaves, roughly chopped

Handful dill sprigs

Finely grated zest and juice of ½ lemon

1 tablespoon sherry vinegar

Preheat the oven to 190°C (375°F).

Place the fish fillets on a board, skin-side up. Gently run the back of a knife down the fish's skin to release any moisture, then pat it dry with paper towel. If you have time, let the fish sit in the fridge, uncovered and skin-side up, for at least 2 hours to further dry out.

In a baking dish, toss the grapes in the extra olive oil and a little salt and pepper. Bake for 10–12 minutes, until the skins are blistered, then transfer to a bowl along with any juices.

Add the olives, almonds, celery, parsley, dill, lemon zest and juice, sherry vinegar and half the remaining olive oil to the bowl. Season lightly with salt and pepper and gently mix, then set aside.

Season both sides of the fish with a little salt. Heat a non-stick frying pan over medium–high heat. Add the remaining olive oil, then carefully add the fish, skin-side down. Season the flesh with pepper, then firmly press down on the fish with the back of a spatula for 10–20 seconds. Cover with a lid, reduce the heat to medium and cook for a further 3–4 minutes. This allows the flesh to cook gently and the skin to become very crispy. Keep a close eye on the fish, as the cooking time may vary slightly, depending on its thickness.

Turn off the heat, flip the fish over and let it rest in the pan for 1–2 minutes. Transfer to a plate and keep warm.

To serve, spoon the grape salad onto serving plates and top with the crispy-skin fish.

Fish in a bag

Cooking fish or seafood in a bag is one of the simplest and most delicious ways to prepare it – perfect for a fast midweek meal. The parcels lock in flavour and moisture, which can be two of the biggest challenges when cooking seafood. This gentle cooking technique is also forgiving enough for novice cooks to try, as it makes it harder to overcook the fish.

For these recipes, use a firm white-fleshed fish such as ling, gemfish, blue-eye trevalla, snapper or barramundi. The instructions are based on 160–180 g (5¾–6⅓ oz) fillets, but they also work with a whole fish – just increase the cooking time to 20–25 minutes. Take your fish out of the fridge 30 minutes before cooking to bring it to room temperature. Each recipe serves four with your choice of sides.

Ginger, soy and spring onion

Thickly slice half a small wombok (Chinese cabbage) and place a handful each in the middle of 4 large pieces of baking paper. Whisk together ⅓ cup (80 ml) soy sauce, 2 tablespoons sesame oil, 2 tablespoons rice vinegar and some grated ginger, and spoon half of this over the cabbage. Lay a seasoned fish fillet, skin-side down, over the cabbage in each parcel and spoon the remaining dressing over the top. Fold the baking paper up and around the fish, rolling the ends up to seal them and form a pouch. Place the pouches on a baking tray and cook in an oven preheated to 210°C (410°F) for 12–15 minutes, then carefully open the parcels, scatter some sliced spring onion (scallion) and coriander (cilantro) leaves over and serve with steamed rice, if desired.

Maple, miso and sesame

Divide 2 bunches broccolini or Asian greens between 4 large pieces of baking paper. In a small bowl, whisk together 2 tablespoons each of white miso, soy sauce, rice vinegar, sesame oil and maple syrup, along with 2 cloves sliced garlic, and pour half of this sauce over the greens. Lay a seasoned fish fillet, skin-side down, over the veggies in each parcel and spoon the remaining sauce over the top. Fold the baking paper up and around the fish, rolling the ends to seal and form a pouch. Place the pouches on a baking tray and cook in an oven preheated to 210°C (410°F) for 12–15 minutes, then carefully open the parcels, scatter some sliced spring onion (scallion) and toasted sesame seeds over and serve with lime wedges and steamed rice, if desired.

White wine, tomato and olive

Slice 3 desiree potatoes into 5 mm (¼ inch) rounds and blanch in a saucepan of lightly salted boiling water, until tender. Divide the cooked potato slices between 4 large pieces of baking paper. Lightly season with salt and pepper and drizzle with a little olive oil. Scatter 5 grape tomatoes around the potato and top with a small handful of roughly chopped silverbeet (Swiss chard) or baby spinach leaves. Lay a seasoned fish fillet, skin-side down, over the spinach in each parcel, drizzle with a little more olive oil, a splash of white wine, 2 tablespoons crushed canned tomatoes, and scatter with some kalamata olives. Fold the baking paper up and around the fish, rolling the ends to seal them and form a pouch. Place the pouches on a baking tray and cook in an oven preheated to 210°C (410°F) for 12–15 minutes. Carefully open the parcels and finish with a squeeze of lemon juice and a handful of dill sprigs and basil leaves scattered over.

15-minute braised squid with chilli, tomatoes and olives

This dish is your go-to for fast midweek cooking. It's light but satisfying, and can be served over steamed rice or couscous, or tossed through your favourite pasta. You could even serve it with some good crusty bread. A simple rocket (arugula) or leaf salad dressed with red wine vinegar and olive oil also works well next to it.

¼ cup (60 ml) olive oil

1 small brown onion, finely chopped

2 cloves garlic, thinly sliced

Generous pinch of dried chilli flakes

Sea salt flakes and ground black pepper

1 x 400 g (14 oz) can baby roma or cherry tomatoes

⅓ cup (55 g) pitted kalamata olives

800 g (1 lb 12 oz) squid tubes and tentacles, cleaned and cut into 2 cm (¾ inch) pieces

1 x 400 g (14 oz) can butter beans, rinsed and drained

2 handfuls baby spinach leaves

Handful flat-leaf parsley leaves, roughly chopped

1 lemon, cut into wedges

Extra virgin olive oil, to drizzle

Good-quality store-bought aioli, to serve (optional)

Place a saucepan over medium–high heat. Add the olive oil, onion, garlic, chilli flakes and a pinch of salt and cook for 3 minutes. Add the tomatoes and olives and cook for a further 3 minutes.

Add the squid tubes and tentacles to the pan, then reduce the heat to a simmer and cook for 5 minutes. Add the butter beans, baby spinach and parsley and mix through.

Serve the squid with the lemon wedges, a drizzle of extra virgin olive oil and some aioli, if you like.

Pro tip Prawns (shrimp), or a firm white-fleshed fish like ling, snapper or blue-eye trevalla, would also work for this recipe.

Moroccan silverbeet and tomato rice

This delicious everyday one-pot wonder is 100 per cent leftovers-approved (LOA). Use other greens like kale or cavolo nero, if you like. For a more substantial version, add some peeled raw prawns (shrimp) or a firm white-fleshed fish in the final 5 minutes of cooking. Another way I like to serve this is with roast eggplant (aubergine) or pumpkin (squash) wedges.

⅓ cup (80 ml) olive oil

1 brown onion, finely chopped

2 cloves garlic, roughly chopped

Sea salt flakes and ground black pepper

2 tablespoons *ras el hanout* (see Notes on page 64)

2 tablespoons harissa paste or fire-roasted chilli salsa (see page 225)

1 small bunch silverbeet (Swiss chard), stalks and all, sliced

2 cups (400 g) long-grain rice, rinsed

1 x 400 g (14 oz) can chopped tomatoes

4 cups (1 litre) vegetable stock

1 x 400 g (14 oz) can chickpeas, rinsed and drained

Handful flat-leaf parsley leaves

Handful mint leaves, roughly chopped

Sumac yoghurt or garlicky whipped tahini (see page 223), or natural Greek-style yoghurt, to serve

1 lemon, cut into wedges, to serve

Place a large, deep frying pan over medium–high heat and add the olive oil, onion, garlic and a pinch of salt. Cook for 3 minutes, stirring continuously, then add the *ras el hanout*, harissa or fire-roasted chilli salsa and silverbeet. Cover with a lid and cook for a further 3 minutes, until the silverbeet is wilted.

Add the rice to the pan and stir through, then add the tomatoes and stock and bring to the boil, continuing to stir for 2 minutes. Adjust the seasoning, add the chickpeas and stir, then reduce the heat to a simmer, cover with a lid and cook for 12 minutes. Remove from the heat and allow the rice to rest for 5 minutes, then stir through the herbs.

To serve, top the rice with the sumac yoghurt, garlicky whipped tahini or yoghurt and a squeeze of lemon juice.

Goes with

· Roasted ling fillet
· Pan-fried tiger prawns (shrimp)
· Pan-fried gemfish fillet

Whole roasted smoked chilli and tamarind fish with sprout salad

Most of the time, cooking whole fish is simpler and more affordable than cooking fillets. Cooking fish on the bone also protects it and helps to lock in moisture. This recipe is great to serve up, family-style, down the middle of the table, letting everyone fill their own lettuce cups. You can use fillets instead of a whole fish, if you like – just reduce the cooking time to about 6–8 minutes.

2 x 500 g (1 lb 2 oz) whole rainbow trout, cleaned *(see Note on page 76)*

Sea salt flakes

⅓ cup (80 ml) smoked chilli and tamarind sauce (see page 228)

Iceberg or butter lettuce cups, to serve

Steamed rice, to serve (optional)

Bean sprout and herb salad

250 g (9 oz) bean sprouts

Iced water

2 handfuls finely shaved wombok (Chinese cabbage) leaves

¼ cup (60 ml) rice vinegar

2 tablespoons soy sauce or tamari

2 tablespoons sesame oil

2 tablespoons sesame seeds, toasted

4 spring onions (scallions), green part only, thinly sliced

2 handfuls coriander (cilantro) leaves

1 long red chilli, thinly sliced

Preheat the oven to 220°C (425°F) and line a large baking tray with baking paper.

Dry the fish inside and out with paper towel and make three shallow cuts down each of its sides. Season well with salt, then drizzle half the smoked chilli and tamarind sauce over it, gently rubbing it in all over. Allow the fish to marinate for 1 hour in the fridge.

Remove the fish from the fridge 30 minutes before cooking to bring it to room temperature and help it cook more evenly. Place it on the tray with its marinade and roast for 15 minutes, until just cooked through (see *pro tip* below).

Meanwhile, make the bean sprout and herb salad. Bring a saucepan of water to the boil and blanch the bean sprouts for 30 seconds. Drain them, then use tongs or a slotted spoon to transfer them to a bowl of iced water to refresh for 1 minute. Gently squeeze them dry and toss with the wombok, rice vinegar, soy sauce or tamari, sesame oil, sesame seeds, two of the spring onions and half the coriander leaves.

Drizzle the remaining smoked chilli and tamarind sauce over the fish. Scatter with the remaining spring onion and coriander, and the sliced chilli. Serve with the bean sprout and herb salad, lettuce cups and steamed rice, if you like.

Pro tip To ensure a whole fish is cooked, check close to the head (its thickest part). The flesh should flake away easily with a fork or small knife.

Whipped pumpkin tahini with scallops, crispy chickpeas and za'atar

This is the pumpkin (squash) version of hummus. It's so sweet and creamy and makes the perfect dip, but is also great with fish and roast veggies. I've popped this in the Autumn chapter but, frankly, I enjoy this all year round.

1 x 400 g (14 oz) can chickpeas, rinsed, drained and dried well on paper towel

⅓ cup (80 ml) olive oil

½ teaspoon curry powder

Sea salt flakes and ground black pepper

1 butternut pumpkin (squash), cut in half lengthways

1 head garlic

½ cup (135 g) hulled tahini

1 teaspoon ground cumin

12 scallops, roe on or off, shell removed

2 tablespoons Calabrian chilli in oil *(see Note on page 60)*, or any other chilli in oil

1 tablespoon extra virgin olive oil

2 tablespoons pomegranate molasses

2 tablespoons dill sprigs, roughly chopped

2 teaspoons black sesame seeds, toasted

2 teaspoons white sesame seeds, toasted

1 tablespoon za'atar

Preheat the oven to 180°C (350°F) and line two baking trays with baking paper.

Toss the chickpeas with 1 tablespoon of the olive oil, the curry powder and a little salt and pepper and scatter them on one of the trays. Place the pumpkin on the second tray. Scoop out any seeds and place them on the tray. Brush the pumpkin and seeds with 2 tablespoons of the olive oil and season with a little salt and pepper. Wrap the whole head of garlic in foil and place it on the tray with the pumpkin.

Transfer both trays to the oven and roast for 30–40 minutes, giving the chickpeas a shake around halfway, until the chickpeas are crisp and the pumpkin is soft and golden. Reserve the pumpkin seeds for garnishing.

Allow the pumpkin and garlic to cool to room temperature, then scoop the pumpkin flesh out (discard the skin) and place in a blender. Squeeze the garlic flesh from the skin and add it to the pumpkin along with the tahini and cumin. Adjust the seasoning, if desired, and blend into a smooth purée, adding a little water if necessary. Set aside.

Place a large frying pan over high heat. Toss the scallops in the remaining olive oil and sear for 20–30 seconds, then flip them and remove from the pan straight away. Transfer to a plate.

Spoon the pumpkin tahini onto a plate and drizzle with the chilli oil, extra virgin olive oil and pomegranate molasses. Finish with the chopped dill, sesame seeds, pumpkin seeds and za'atar, and top with the scallops and crispy chickpeas.

Pomegranate ezme

'Ezme' is the Turkish word for 'mashed' or 'crushed'. It's also the name of this addictive finely chopped Turkish salad. There are many versions of it, and this is mine – perhaps not entirely traditional, but so delicious. Something magical happens to vegetables when they're chopped finely: more flavour seems to burst out, making them very exciting to eat.

This salad is amazing served with any grilled fish and creamy babaganoush. It will keep overnight in the fridge, and the quantities can easily be increased to feed a crowd.

2 vine-ripened tomatoes, deseeded and finely chopped

1 red capsicum (pepper), finely chopped

1 small red onion, finely chopped

Seeds from ½ pomegranate

¼ cup (40 g) pitted kalamata olives, roughly chopped

½ cup (10 g) flat-leaf parsley leaves, finely chopped

½ cup (30 g) dill sprigs, roughly chopped

1 clove garlic, finely chopped or crushed

Juice of 1 lemon

¼ cup (60 ml) extra virgin olive oil

1 tablespoon pomegranate molasses

1 teaspoon ground cumin (optional)

Sea salt flakes and ground black pepper

Combine all the ingredients in a bowl, season to taste and mix well. Allow to stand for at least 20 minutes at room temperature, or for up to two hours in the fridge, to let the flavours develop. If the salad is marinating in the fridge, bring it to room temperature before serving.

Goes with

·   Grilled whole leatherjacket
·   Grilled kingfish fillet
·   Seared albacore tuna fillet

Sri Lankan-inspired fish curry

I love this curry, because it's so versatile and a great way to try different types of fish. Leatherjacket is such an underrated fish and delicious when gently poached in a curry such as this one. It's also very easy to make this plant-based by swapping in roast eggplant (aubergine) or cauliflower instead of fish.

The tamarind is what makes this dish – it's one of my favourite ingredients to have in the pantry.

¼ cup (60 ml) coconut oil

3 sprigs fresh curry leaves

1 small brown onion, chopped

2 cloves garlic, finely chopped

2 tablespoons *ras el hanout* (see Note on page 64)

2 sweet potatoes (kumara), peeled and cut into 3 cm (1¼ inch) chunks

1 cup (200 g) canned chopped tomatoes

2 cups (500 ml) vegetable stock

2 tablespoons tamarind concentrate (see Notes)

1 cup (250 ml) coconut milk

2 whole leatherjackets, bream or snapper, cleaned (see Note on page 76), weighing approximately 1 kg (2 lb 4 oz)

2 handfuls baby spinach leaves

Coriander (cilantro) leaves, to serve

Lime wedges, to serve

Steamed basmati rice or warmed roti, to serve

Coconut sambal

Handful coriander (cilantro) leaves, roughly chopped

½ cup (35 g) shredded coconut, lightly toasted

Juice of 1 lime

Sea salt flakes

½ long green chilli, deseeded and thinly sliced (see Notes)

To make the coconut sambal, mix all the ingredients in a bowl until combined. Taste and lightly season with more salt, if required. Set aside.

Place a large, deep frying pan over medium–high heat and add the coconut oil and 2 sprigs of curry leaves. Cook for 10–15 seconds, until crisp, then use tongs to carefully transfer to paper towel to drain. Set aside.

Add the onion and garlic to the pan with a pinch of salt and cook until soft, then add the *ras el hanout*, sweet potato and the remaining curry leaf sprig and continue stirring for 2 minutes. Add the tomatoes and cook for 1 minute, then add the vegetable stock and tamarind concentrate and bring to the boil.

Reduce the heat to a simmer, cover the pan with a lid and cook, stirring occasionally, for 10 minutes, until the sweet potato starts to soften.

Add the coconut milk and fish, cover again and poach for 8 minutes, until just cooked. Gently stir through the baby spinach until wilted, being careful not to break the fish.

Top the curry with the crispy curry leaves, coconut sambal and coriander and serve with the lime wedges, steamed basmati rice or warmed roti alongside.

Notes Tamarind concentrate is available at some supermarkets and most Asian grocers.

If you don't like too much heat, leave the chilli out of the sambal.

Pro tip You can make the curry base and sambal up to 3 days in advance and then reheat them when you need to.

King salmon biryani

I love everything about this dish. You're packing so much flavour into one pot, layering up the rice, onion, herbs and spices, which all help to gently cook the fish. I love butter chicken spice mix (not entirely traditional, but so delicious), but you can use any spice mix you like. It might seem like there are a few steps involved, but it really comes together easily.

This dish, which happens to be leftovers-approved (LOA), also offers the opportunity to try different fish types – just stick to firmer white-fleshed fish, ocean trout or Spanish mackerel.

1 cup (260 g) natural Greek-style yoghurt

1 tablespoon butter chicken spice mix (or any spice mix), plus 2 teaspoons extra

¼ cup (60 ml) olive oil

Finely grated zest of 1 lime

1 x 800 g (1 lb 12 oz) or 2 x 400 g (14 oz) NZ king salmon fillets

Sea salt flakes and ground black pepper

3 brown onions, thinly sliced

2 cups (400 g) basmati rice, rinsed

4 cardamom pods

6 whole cloves

1 cinnamon stick

2 fresh or dried bay leaves

Handful coriander (cilantro) leaves, roughly chopped

Handful mint leaves, roughly chopped

Large pinch of saffron threads soaked in ½ cup (125 ml) water

Tomato, red onion and coriander (cilantro) salad, to serve

Lime halves, to serve

Avocado tzatziki (see page 99), to serve (optional)

Combine the yoghurt with the spice mix, 1 tablespoon of the olive oil and the lime zest. Place the salmon in a large dish or tray, season with salt and pepper, then spoon the yoghurt marinade over the fish and gently rub it in all over. Refrigerate for 2–3 hours or overnight to marinate, then bring it out of the fridge 30 minutes before cooking to bring it to room temperature.

Place the onion in a saucepan with the remaining olive oil and a good pinch of salt. Stir, cover with a lid and cook over medium heat for 10 minutes, until the onion begins to caramelise. Remove the lid and cook for a further 5 minutes, stirring until deeply caramelised. Set aside.

Bring a saucepan of water to the boil with 2 teaspoons salt. Add the rice, cardamom, cloves, cinnamon and bay leaves and bring to the boil. Cook for 4 minutes, then drain the rice and set aside.

Preheat the oven to 220°C (425°F). Place the marinated salmon, skin-side down, and any remaining marinade in a large, deep ovenproof dish or pot. Combine the rice with the onion, herbs (reserving a quarter for garnish) and extra spice mix and spoon this over the salmon. Drizzle the saffron-infused water evenly over the rice. Place a piece of baking paper over the rice to cover it, then cover with a lid or a layer of foil.

Bake the rice in the oven for 25–30 minutes, then allow it to rest for 5 minutes. Remove the lid and scatter on the remaining herbs.

Serve the biryani with the tomato, red onion and coriander salad, lime halves and the avocado tzatziki, if desired.

Pro tip You can make the caramelised onion and marinate the fish the day before.

**Party pumpkin
with jewelled rice
and yoghurt**
Pages 162–163

Party pumpkin with jewelled rice and yoghurt

This stunning dish is perfect for when you want some plant-based wow factor. It may seem like there are a few steps, but they can easily be done while the pumpkin (squash) roasts. Then all that's left to do is combine everything, sit down with your family or friends and dig in! Enjoy this on its own or with any of the other veggie dishes from this book, some babaganoush (page 229) and a beautiful whole roasted fish. It also keeps well in the fridge for leftovers, which is an added bonus.

1 small pumpkin (squash), such as kent, cut in half crossways

½ cup (75 g) pistachio nuts

½ cup (65 g) slivered almonds

½ cup (125 ml) olive oil

Sea salt flakes and ground black pepper

1 carrot, cut into matchsticks

1 tablespoon caster (superfine) sugar

2 tablespoons white wine vinegar

2 cups (400 g) basmati rice, rinsed

½ teaspoon saffron threads

2 brown onions, thinly sliced

1½ tablespoons *ras el hanout* (see Notes on page 64)

1 cup (170 g) golden raisins

Seeds from 1 pomegranate

Finely grated zest of 1 orange

½ bunch coriander (cilantro), leaves picked and finely chopped, plus extra whole leaves, to serve

2 cups (520 g) natural Greek-style yoghurt

Pomegranate molasses, to drizzle

Preheat the oven to 210°C (410°F) and line two baking trays with baking paper.

Scoop the seeds out of the pumpkin, separating them from any flesh. Combine the pumpkin seeds with the nuts and 1 tablespoon of the olive oil and scatter on one of the trays. Roast for 7 minutes, until toasted, and set aside.

Place the pumpkin on the second tray and brush it with ¼ cup (60 ml) of the olive oil. Season well with salt and pepper and roast for 1 hour, until soft when pierced with a knife. Set aside.

Place the carrot in a small bowl with the sugar, a pinch of salt and the vinegar. Allow to stand for at least 15 minutes to macerate.

Place the rice and saffron in a small saucepan and cover with 3 cups (750 ml) water and a pinch of salt. Bring to the boil, then reduce the heat to low, cover with a lid and cook for 10 minutes. Remove from the heat and allow it to stand for 10 minutes, then spoon the rice into a bowl and allow it to cool slightly.

Goes with

· Whole roasted snapper
· Roasted blue-eye trevalla fillet
· Pan-fried NZ king salmon fillet

Meanwhile, place the onion, the remaining olive oil and a good pinch of salt in a small saucepan. Cover with a lid and cook over low heat for 5 minutes, until the onion is soft, then increase the heat, remove the lid and cook, stirring often, for a further 5–7 minutes, until the onion begins to caramelise. Add the *ras el hanout* in the final minute of cooking and stir until fragrant. Set aside.

Combine the rice with the nuts, pumpkin seeds, raisins, caramelised onion, pickled carrot, pomegranate, orange zest and coriander. Season to taste, if you like, and mix well.

Spoon the yoghurt over the pumpkin and drizzle with the pomegranate molasses. Spoon the jewelled rice on top, finish with the extra coriander and serve.

Moroccan couscous capsicums

These capsicums (peppers) are stand-alone stars any night of the week, but they also work really well with grilled, pan-fried or roasted fish. The couscous is also a great salad in its own right, or paired with some grilled seafood or roast veggies.

4 large mixed colour capsicums (peppers)

⅓ cup (80 ml) olive oil

Sea salt flakes and ground black pepper

2 cups (380 g) couscous

2 cups (500 ml) vegetable stock

1–2 tablespoons fire-roasted chilli salsa (see page 225), or store-bought harissa, plus extra to serve

Finely grated zest and juice of 1 lemon

½ cup (65 g) slivered almonds, toasted

8 fresh dates, roughly chopped

1 x 400 g (14 oz) can chickpeas, rinsed and drained well

Handful coriander leaves, roughly chopped

Handful mint leaves, roughly chopped

1 cup (260 g) natural Greek-style yoghurt, to serve

Preheat the oven to 190°C (375°F).

Cut the capsicums in half lengthways, scoop out the seeds and discard. Place the capsicum halves, cut-side up, on a baking tray, drizzle with 2 tablespoons of the olive oil and season with salt and pepper. Roast for 7 minutes, until they begin to soften, then set aside.

Place the couscous in a heatproof bowl. Pour the stock into a small saucepan over medium heat and bring to the boil. Add the fire-roasted chilli salsa or harissa, then pour it over the couscous. Cover with a plate and allow it to steam and absorb the stock for 10 minutes.

Using a fork, fluff up the couscous, then dress it with the remaining olive oil and the lemon zest and juice. Add the almonds, dates, chickpeas and herbs and mix through, adjusting the seasoning to taste.

Fill the capsicum halves with the couscous mixture. Swirl the yoghurt and extra fire-roasted chilli salsa or harissa together and spoon it over the top before serving.

Goes with

· Pan-fried bream fillet
· Grilled ling skewers
· Grilled tiger prawns (shrimp)

Mushroom and kimchi fried brown rice with miso fish

This delicious fried rice is on the table in 10 minutes, which is less time than it takes to order take-away. For a completely plant-based version, leave out the egg and add a bunch of roughly chopped broccolini and a handful of edamame beans at the end, or make miso eggplant (aubergine) to enjoy with it (see the *pro tip* below).

400 g (14 oz) firm-fleshed, skinless fish fillet, such as blue-eye trevalla, gemfish, ocean trout or NZ king salmon

¼ cup (60 ml) sesame oil

3 cups (250 g) mixed mushrooms, such as enoki, oyster, shiitake or king brown, sliced

Sea salt flakes

2 cloves garlic, thinly sliced

2 free-range eggs

4 cups (840 g) cooked and cooled brown rice

1 cup (200 g) kimchi, roughly chopped

3 spring onions (scallions), thinly sliced

2 tablespoons black sesame seeds

1 iceberg lettuce, separated into 12 lettuce cups

Miso glaze

2 tablespoons white miso

2 tablespoons maple syrup or honey

1 tablespoon finely grated ginger

1 tablespoon rice vinegar

1 tablespoon sesame oil

To make the miso glaze, combine all the ingredients in a bowl. Pour it over the fish, coating it well. At this stage, you could either leave the fish at room temperature for up to 30 minutes to marinate, or refrigerate it overnight and remove from the fridge 30 minutes before cooking.

Preheat the oven to 200°C (400°F) and line a baking tray with baking paper.

Place the marinated fish on the tray and roast for 6–8 minutes, depending on its thickness. You want it to just begin to flake with a fork or small knife.

Place a wok or frying pan over high heat and add half the sesame oil, the mushrooms and a pinch of salt. Stir-fry for 2 minutes, then add half the garlic in the last 30 seconds of cooking and stir through. Transfer to a plate.

Place the cleaned wok or pan over high heat once more and add the remaining sesame oil, garlic and the eggs. Scramble the eggs with a wooden spoon, then add the rice and stir-fry until it starts to sizzle slightly. Add the kimchi and stir-fry for 1 minute, then add two-thirds of the spring onion and toss through.

Spoon the fried rice onto a plate and top with the sesame seeds and the remaining spring onion. Serve with the fish and lettuce, letting everyone spoon the rice and fish into their lettuce cups before digging in.

Pro tip The miso glaze works so well on eggplant (aubergine). Simply cut the eggplant in half lengthways, brush it with a little olive oil, season and roast at 210°C (410°F) for 15 minutes, then spread the glaze over it, turn the heat in your oven right up and roast for a further 3–5 minutes, until caramelised.

Autumn harvest bowl

This simple and nourishing bowl is all-time! Just one tray and one bowl are all that are called for to create layers of flavour. Coated in a creamy tahini dressing, with bursts of pomegranate throughout, this salad is so tasty for lunch, dinner, and again the next day.

To keep things interesting, try other veggies like eggplant (aubergine), pumpkin (squash) or cauliflower, and mix up the sauces using the ones in the Arsenal of Flavours (page 219).

2 large sweet potatoes (kumara), cut into pieces

500 g (1 lb 2 oz) brussels sprouts, cut in half

2 brown onions, cut into thick wedges

¼ cup (60 ml) olive oil

Sea salt flakes and ground black pepper

1 cup (180 g) farro

½ bunch flat-leaf parsley, leaves picked and roughly chopped

1 x 400 g (14 oz) can chickpeas, rinsed and drained

Seeds from ½ pomegranate

½ bunch mint, leaves picked

2 tablespoons sherry vinegar

Juice of 1 lemon

¼ cup (60 ml) extra virgin olive oil

1 tablespoon za'atar

1 cup (280 g) garlicky whipped tahini or sumac yoghurt (see page 223), or green goddess tahini sauce (see page 222), to serve

Preheat the oven to 210°C (410°F) and line a baking tray with baking paper.

Combine the sweet potato, brussels sprouts and onion in a bowl and dress with the olive oil and a little salt and pepper. Scatter on the baking tray and roast for 20–25 minutes, until caramelised.

Meanwhile, bring a saucepan of water to the boil and add the farro. Cook for 15 minutes or until al dente, then drain and cool.

Combine the roast veggies with the parsley, chickpeas, farro, pomegranate and mint. Season to taste and dress with the vinegar, lemon juice and extra virgin olive oil. Serve topped with the za'atar and garlicky whipped tahini, sumac yoghurt or green goddess tahini sauce.

Pro tip Roast the veggies and cook the farro ahead of time and keep them at room temperature. Then simply mix and dress everything when you're ready to serve. Oh, and make extra for an easy lunch the next day!

Goes with

· Roasted NZ king salmon fillet
· Roasted gemfish fillet
· Pan-fried barramundi fillet

Chopped broccoli, red rice and goat's cheese salad

We make this dish often, as it goes with everything and is so satisfying. It's perfect for everyday lunches, dinners or picnics, and pairs with just about any seafood.

If you can't find red rice, swap it with brown or basmati rice, quinoa, or any grain of your choice.

1½ cups (315 g) red rice, washed

Sea salt flakes

2 large heads broccoli

2 tablespoons olive oil

Generous pinch of dried chilli flakes

½ bunch flat-leaf parsley, leaves picked and roughly chopped

½ bunch mint, leaves picked and roughly chopped

2 spring onions (scallions), green part only, thinly sliced

Handful pepitas (pumpkin seeds), toasted

Handful sunflower seeds, toasted

Handful broccoli sprouts

Juice of 1 lemon

1 tablespoon sherry or red wine vinegar

⅓ cup (80 ml) extra virgin olive oil

100 g (3½ oz) goat's cheese or marinated feta

Place the red rice in a saucepan, add 3 cups (750 ml) water and a pinch of salt and bring to the boil. Stir and cover with a lid, then reduce the heat to low and cook for 20 minutes. Turn the heat off and allow the rice to steam for 5 minutes, then spoon into a bowl to cool. Set aside.

Preheat the oven to 220°C (425°F) and line a large baking tray with baking paper.

Cut the broccoli florets and stalks into large pieces, then toss with the olive oil, chilli flakes and a generous pinch of salt. Place on the tray and cook for 8 minutes, until the broccoli is a little charred but still bright green. Remove from the oven, allow to cool slightly, then roughly chop the florets and stalks. Add them to the rice along with the parsley, mint, spring onion, seeds and sprouts.

Dress the salad with the lemon juice, vinegar and extra virgin olive oil. Season with salt and pepper and gently toss to combine. Crumble the goat's cheese or feta over the top and gently fold through a couple more times before serving.

Goes with

· Whole roasted rainbow trout
· Seared albacore tuna fillet
· Pan-fried snapper fillet

Suquet

This dish has humble origins – it was made by Catalan fishermen as a way to use up the seafood they were unable to sell that day. It's simple to prepare, with a big return on flavour. Traditionally served as a communal dish to share around the table, *suquet* is a celebration of seasonal seafood. I fell in love with it while travelling through Catalonia. Like all good regional dishes, it varies depending on who's cooking it, but it's centred around the abundant seafood that Catalonia is known for.

100 ml (3½ fl oz) olive oil

3 cloves garlic, sliced

½ cup (80 g) blanched almonds

Sea salt flakes

Handful flat-leaf parsley leaves, finely chopped

1 small brown onion, finely chopped

¼ cup (60 ml) tomato paste (concentrated purée)

Pinch of sweet smoked paprika

4 fresh bay leaves

2 red-skinned potatoes, such as desiree, peeled and sliced into 5 mm (¼ inch) rounds

1 cup (250 ml) dry white wine

Pinch of saffron threads (optional)

1 x 400 g (14 oz) can crushed tomatoes

2 cups (500 ml) chicken or fish stock

300 g (10½ oz) ling or blue-eye trevalla fillet, diced

8 raw king prawns (shrimp), heads on and tails intact

500 g (1 lb 2 oz) mussels, scrubbed and debearded

Crusty bread, to serve (optional)

Place a small frying pan over medium heat and add 2 tablespoons of the olive oil, the garlic, almonds and a pinch of salt. Cook, stirring constantly, until the garlic is lightly caramelised. Transfer the mixture to a mortar and pestle to cool, then crush it until it resembles rough breadcrumbs. Stir through the parsley and set aside.

Heat a large saucepan over medium–high heat and add the remaining olive oil, the onion and a good pinch of salt. Cook, stirring often, for 5 minutes, until the onion is translucent but not coloured.

Add the tomato paste, paprika, bay leaves and potato and stir through, then continue to cook for 2 minutes. Add the wine and saffron (if using) and cook for a further 2 minutes, then add the crushed tomatoes and stock. Reduce the heat to a simmer and cook for 10 minutes, until the potato is almost cooked.

Add the fish to the pan and gently poach it for 2 minutes, then add the prawns and mussels. Cover with the lid and cook for 5 minutes or until cooked.

Spoon the almond and onion mixture over the *suquet* and serve with some crusty bread, if you like.

WINTER

Miso mushrooms in a bag

This simple yet impressive dish is ready in 30 minutes. The miso dressing is one you always need in your fridge – you'll soon be using it in many other veggie and fish dishes.

If you want to add fish to this, simply place 150 g (5½ oz) firm white-fleshed fish or ocean trout that has been seasoned and marinated in the miso marinade over the mushrooms, then wrap it all up. There's also the option of pan-frying or roasting the fish and serving it separately.

600 g (1 lb 5 oz) mixed mushrooms, sliced

Steamed rice and steamed Asian greens or broccolini, to serve

3 spring onions (scallions), thinly sliced, to serve

2 tablespoons toasted sesame seeds, to serve

Miso dressing

¼ cup (70 g) white miso

½ cup (125 ml) rice vinegar

2 tablespoons maple syrup or honey

2 tablespoons soy sauce

2 tablespoons sesame oil

2 cloves garlic, crushed

Preheat the oven to 200°C (400°F).

Place the mushrooms in a bowl.

To make the miso dressing, mix all the ingredients together and then pour over the mushrooms.

Cut four large rectangles of baking paper, then place one sheet on top of another to make two rectangular stacks. Divide the mushrooms and dressing between each paper stack, then bring the edges up to make two shallow bowl shapes. Tie the ends together with some string to form two money bags. Alternatively, you could also fold the bags closed and then wrap them in foil to enclose.

Place the mushroom bags on a baking tray and bake for 15–20 minutes.

Meanwhile, spoon the rice into serving bowls and top with the steamed greens, spring onion and sesame seeds.

Remove the bags from the oven, cut the strings open, and serve the mushrooms in the middle of the table, letting everyone spoon some over their rice and greens, along with plenty of the delicious miso broth.

Goes with

· Pan-fried blue-eye trevalla
· Roasted NZ king salmon
· Bag-cooked ling fillet

Gochujang fish and brussels sprouts tray bake

Brussels sprouts work so well in this dish, but feel free to mix it up with other seasonal veggies like cauliflower, broccoli, pumpkin (squash), eggplant (aubergine) or zucchini (courgette), cut into similar-sized pieces. Serve this with steamed rice or grains, or throw some diced sweet potato (kumara) onto the tray before roasting.

650 g (1 lb 7 oz) blue-eye trevalla or ling fillet, skin on

500 g (1 lb 2 oz) brussels sprouts, cut in half

1 brown onion, cut into thin wedges

1 bunch broccolini

Sea salt flakes

2 tablespoons olive oil

1 cup (250 ml) gochujang dressing (see page 228)

4 radishes, thinly sliced

3 spring onions (scallions), thinly sliced

½ cup (75 g) edamame beans

1 tablespoon rice vinegar

1 tablespoon sesame oil

½ cup (100 g) kimchi, to serve (optional)

Steamed rice, to serve

Preheat the oven to 230°C (450°F).

Place the fish in a shallow bowl. Place the brussels sprouts and onion in a second bowl and the broccolini in a third bowl. Season them all with a little salt, drizzle with the olive oil and divide the gochujang dressing between the three bowls, reserving ¼ cup (60 ml) of the dressing for serving. Gently toss all the ingredients together in their separate bowls to coat them.

Scatter the brussels sprouts, onion and any remaining marinade onto a large baking tray lined with baking paper and roast for 7 minutes. Remove from the oven and add the fish, skin-side down, the broccolini and all the marinade from the bowls. Roast for 8 minutes, until the fish is just cooked and the veggies are a little charred and gnarly.

Meanwhile, combine the radish, spring onion and edamame with the rice vinegar, sesame oil and a little salt. Scatter this over the fish and veggies and serve with the kimchi, the reserved gochujang dressing and the steamed rice.

Veggie lasagne with mushroom and lentil ragu

This veggie lasagne has cult status in our house. It also happens to be leftovers-approved (LOA). You can make the mushroom and lentil ragu ahead of time, even up to a day or two earlier. Other veggies, like pumpkin (squash) or sweet potato (kumara), can be used in place of the ones listed. I use rice instead of the traditional pasta sheets, as it soaks up all the delicious juices from the veggies and creates another amazing layer. If you want to keep it light, just leave out the rice.

½ cup (125 ml) olive oil

1 brown onion, finely chopped

2 cloves garlic, finely chopped

Sea salt flakes and ground black pepper

4 large flat or 12 button mushrooms, finely chopped

2 tablespoons tomato paste (concentrated purée)

Pinch of dried chilli flakes (optional)

1 x 400 g (14 oz) can crushed tomatoes

1 x 400 g (14 oz) can cherry tomatoes

1¼ cups (310 ml) vegetable stock or water

2 x 400 g (14 oz) can lentils, rinsed and drained

½ cup (100 g) long-grain rice (optional)

2 eggplants (aubergines), cut into 1 cm (½ inch) thick slices

4 zucchinis (courgettes), thinly sliced

Handful parsley leaves

Handful basil leaves

Grated parmesan or crumbled feta, to serve (optional)

Leaf salad, to serve (optional)

Heat 2 tablespoons of the olive oil in a large frying pan over medium–high heat and add the onion, garlic and a good pinch of salt and pepper. Cook for 5 minutes, until soft, then add the mushrooms, tomato paste and chilli flakes (if using) and cook for a further 2–3 minutes, stirring occasionally.

Add the crushed tomatoes, cherry tomatoes and stock, reduce the heat to a simmer and cook for 20 minutes, stirring occasionally, then add the lentils and cook for a further 2 minutes. Season to taste.

Preheat the oven to 200°C (400°F).

Spoon one-third of the mushroom ragu into a large baking dish and top with half the rice. Cover with all the sliced eggplant, season with salt and pepper and drizzle with 2 tablespoons of the olive oil. Spoon another third of the ragu over the eggplant, followed by the remaining rice, and then a layer of zucchini. Season again and drizzle with the remaining olive oil. Finish with a layer of the remaining ragu, then cover with baking paper and a layer of foil to enclose. Bake for 1 hour, until the eggplant is soft when pierced with a knife.

Serve with the parsley and basil scattered over, and some parmesan or feta and a leaf salad, if desired.

Goes with

· Pan-fried mirror dory fillet
· Roasted whole rainbow trout
· Grilled kingfish fillet

Caramelised cauliflower salad with dates, almonds and buckwheat

Roast cauliflower is probably my favourite salad staple. Swap the buckwheat for any other grain, brown rice or lentils, and switch dates with sultanas, cranberries, diced apple or pomegranate, if you like. This salad can be made up to 2 hours ahead of time and refrigerated without the dressing.

1 small cauliflower, cut into florets

1 brown onion, cut into thick wedges

1 teaspoon ground cumin seeds

1 teaspoon ground coriander seeds

⅓ cup (80 ml) olive oil

Sea salt flakes and ground black pepper

1 cup (195 g) buckwheat, soaked overnight and drained

8 fresh dates, roughly torn

¼ cup (40 g) toasted almonds, roughly chopped

3 celery sticks, thinly sliced

Handful flat-leaf parsley leaves

Handful mint leaves

Handful dill sprigs

2 tablespoons extra virgin olive oil

1 tablespoon red wine vinegar

Preheat the oven to 220°C (425°F) and line a baking tray with baking paper.

Bring a saucepan of water to the boil.

Meanwhile, toss the cauliflower and onion in a bowl with the spices, olive oil and some salt and pepper. Scatter on the tray and roast for around 15 minutes, until charred and tender. Set aside.

Rinse the buckwheat well, then drain it again. Blanch it in the boiling water for 4 minutes, then refresh under cold running water and drain it well again. Place it in a bowl with the roasted cauliflower and onion, the dates, almonds, celery and herbs.

Dress the salad with the extra virgin olive oil, vinegar and some salt and pepper, and gently toss to combine before serving.

Goes with

- Roasted whole rainbow trout
- Pan-fried mirror dory fillet
- Roasted whole barramundi

Fish pot pie

This is a super-simple pot pie that you can whip up any night of the week. Serve it with a leaf salad or my raw winter slaw (page 200) and some roast potatoes. It can also be made the day before and stored, covered and uncooked, in the fridge until you're ready to bake it. Feel free to use whatever fish is available to you at the time. Prawns (shrimp) and scallops would add some luxe factor. The cavolo nero can be swapped with a large bunch of English spinach – just drain the spinach well after it's cooked, otherwise the pie will be too watery.

2 tablespoons olive oil

2 tablespoons red onion, finely chopped

¼ bunch cavolo nero leaves, finely chopped

Sea salt flakes and ground black pepper

2 tablespoons baby capers, rinsed and drained

2 tablespoons finely chopped cornichons

¼ cup (15 g) dill sprigs, roughly chopped

¼ cup (5 g) flat-leaf parsley leaves, finely chopped

Finely grated zest of 1 lemon

1 cup (245 g) crème fraiche or thick (double) cream

600 g (1 lb 5 oz) ling fillet, or another firm white-fleshed fish, such as blue-eye trevalla, snapper or hake, cut into 3 cm (1¼ inch) pieces

600 g (1 lb 5 oz) skinless ocean trout fillet, cut into 3 cm (1¼ inch) pieces

1 cup (140 g) frozen peas, thawed

1 sheet good-quality store-bought butter puff pastry

1 egg yolk, lightly whisked

Preheat the oven to 210°C (410°F).

Heat a frying pan over medium–high heat and add the olive oil, onion, cavolo nero and a pinch of salt. Stir well, cover with a lid and cook for 3 minutes, then remove the lid and cook for a further 2–3 minutes, stirring often, until all the liquid evaporates. You don't want any liquid remaining, otherwise the pie will be too wet.

Transfer the cavolo nero to a bowl and allow it to cool, then add the baby capers, cornichon, herbs, lemon zest, crème fraiche or cream, fish and peas. Season well and fold through to combine.

Spoon the pie filling into a shallow 30 cm x 20 cm (12 inch x 8 inch) pie dish. A similar-sized round or oval dish would also work. Cover with the puff pastry, trimming and tucking the edges to secure the filling tightly, then brush the pastry with the egg yolk. Make a hole in the middle to allow steam to escape and sprinkle with a little salt. Bake for around 25 minutes, until the pastry is golden. Serve hot.

Grilled broccoli cutlets with freekeh and sumac yoghurt

Cutting the broccoli into wedges, which I like to call 'cutlets', means nothing is wasted and makes it the true hero of the dish. I've used freekeh here, but you could use any other grain, or even lentils. Cooked grains can last in the fridge for up to 4 days and can help bring a meal together so easily, so I always like to have some on hand.

1½ cups (330 g) freekeh

½ cup (80 g) almonds, toasted and chopped

2 tablespoons pepitas (pumpkin seeds)

⅓ cup (60 g) golden raisins, roughly chopped

Handful flat-leaf parsley leaves, roughly chopped

Handful mint leaves, roughly chopped

2 spring onions (scallions), thinly sliced

2 large heads broccoli

2 tablespoons olive oil

Sea salt flakes and ground black pepper

¼ cup (60 ml) zhoug (see page 224), or use a store-bought dairy-free pesto

Juice of 1 lemon

¼ cup (60 ml) extra virgin olive oil

1 tablespoon red wine vinegar

1 tablespoon pomegranate molasses

1 cup (275 g) sumac yoghurt or garlicky whipped tahini (see page 223), to serve

Bring a saucepan of water to the boil. Add the freekeh and cook for 12–15 minutes, until al dente. Drain and allow to cool, then place in a serving bowl or tray with the almonds, pepitas, raisins, herbs and spring onion. Mix to combine, then set aside.

Cut each head of broccoli lengthways into six even pieces to create 'cutlets' and toss with the olive oil, salt and pepper in a heatproof bowl.

Preheat a barbecue or char-grill pan to medium–high.

Grill the broccoli cutlets for 6 minutes, turning to cook all sides evenly. Return to the bowl and gently mix with the zhoug, lemon juice and a splash of the extra virgin olive oil.

Dress the freekeh salad with the vinegar, pomegranate molasses and the remaining extra virgin olive oil. Season to taste.

To serve, place the broccoli cutlets on top of the freekeh and follow with a generous spoonful of sumac yoghurt or garlicky whipped tahini.

Goes with

· Grilled kingfish fillet
· Pan-fried blue-eye trevalla fillet
· Whole roasted rainbow trout

Whole roasted golden goddess cauliflower

Not a week goes by that we don't make a whole roasted cauliflower of some sort – it's one of the tastiest and most affordable centrepieces for your table. This is just as delicious served at room temperature, so don't rush to get it out hot. If you can't find black barley, use any other grain.

Refrigerate the rest of the turmeric sauce for up to 1 week, and use it to dial up the most humble of salads or roast veggies.

Sea salt flakes and ground black pepper

1 large cauliflower

1½ cups (330 g) black barley (see Note)

2 tablespoons olive oil

Sea salt flakes and ground black pepper

Handful coriander (cilantro) leaves

Handful dill sprigs

Handful mint leaves

2 spring onions (scallions), thinly sliced

2 tablespoons red wine vinegar

⅓ cup (80 ml) extra virgin olive oil

¼ cup (40 g) macadamia and lemon myrtle dukkah (see page 231, or use any good-quality store-bought dukkah)

Turmeric tahini golden goddess sauce

⅓ cup (90 g) hulled tahini

Juice of 1 lemon

1 tablespoon olive oil

1 tablespoon maple syrup or honey

½ teaspoon ground turmeric

Bring a large saucepan of water to the boil. Add 2 tablespoons salt and the whole cauliflower and simmer for 15 minutes.

Meanwhile, bring another saucepan of water to the boil, add the barley and cook for 15 minutes or until al dente. Drain the barley, rinse it under cold water and drain it well again. Place it in a bowl and set aside.

Preheat the oven to 230°C (450°F) and line a baking tray with baking paper.

Carefully transfer the cauliflower to a colander and allow it to drain for around 10 minutes.

Place the cauliflower on the tray, brush or drizzle with the olive oil and season with salt and pepper. Roast for 25–30 minutes, until golden, then allow to cool for 15 minutes.

Roughly chop half the herbs and add to the barley with the spring onion, vinegar and extra virgin olive oil. Season with salt and pepper to taste and set aside.

To make the turmeric tahini golden goddess sauce, whisk all the ingredients with ⅓ cup (80 ml) water and season to taste.

To serve, place the cauliflower on a large serving plate and spoon the barley around it. Drizzle with ½ cup of the turmeric tahini golden goddess sauce, then top with the dukkah and the remaining herbs.

Note You can find black barley at most greengrocers and health food stores. If you can't find it, use freekeh, farro, quinoa, brown or red rice.

Pro tip Poach the cauliflower, make the sauce and cook the barley in advance, if you like, so all that's left to do is roast the cauli and assemble before serving.

Goes with

· Roasted NZ king salmon fillet
· Grilled kingfish fillet
· Whole roasted rainbow trout

A bag of gnarly carrots

I love turning a humble bag of carrots into the most delicious, gnarly delights. Enjoy the spicy roast carrots below as a veggie side, or transform them into three amazing dishes. Each serves four people as a light meal or as part of a larger spread. If you don't like the spice factor, simply leave out the salsa or harissa.

Spicy roast carrots

Toss 1 kg (2 lb 4 oz) washed carrots with 2 tablespoons fire-roasted chilli salsa (see page 225) or harissa, 1 tablespoon *ras el hanout* (*see Notes on page 64*), ⅓ cup (80 ml) olive oil and a little salt, then place on a baking tray lined with baking paper. Cover with baking paper and foil and roast in an oven preheated to 200°C (400°F) for 50 minutes, until soft. Serve the carrots as they are, or in one of the following tasty creations.

Crushed carrots with feta, black barley and preserved lemon

Roughly mash the spicy roast carrots with a fork and place in a bowl with any remaining oil from the roasting tray plus 1 cup (200 g) cooked black barley, ⅓ cup (60 g) thinly sliced preserved lemon skin, a handful each of chopped mint and coriander (cilantro) leaves, the juice of 1 lemon and ¼ cup (60 ml) extra virgin olive oil. Season with salt and pepper and gently toss to combine. Top with 100 g (3½ oz) crumbled marinated feta and 1 tablespoon za'atar, and a drizzle of pomegranate molasses.

Roast carrot, coconut and miso soup

Thickly slice 3 spicy roast carrots and set aside. Place the remaining carrots in a blender with any remaining spicy oil from the roasting tray and 1 cup (250 ml) vegetable stock, then blend into a smooth thick purée. Pour the mixture into a saucepan over medium heat, then add 5 cups (1.25 litres) vegetable stock, 1¼ cups (310 ml) coconut milk and 2 tablespoons white miso. Once hot, season to taste, then ladle the soup into four bowls and top with the reserved sliced carrots and 100 ml (3½ fl oz) coconut milk. Sprinkle with some macadamia and lemon myrtle dukkah (see page 231) or any good-quality store-bought dukkah, and a handful of coriander (cilantro) leaves.

Spicy carrots with maple, pepitas, yoghurt and mint

While the spicy roast carrots are still on the tray, drizzle them with 2 tablespoons maple syrup and sprinkle with the finely grated zest of 1 lemon and a handful each of mint leaves and dill sprigs. Toss to combine. Spoon 1 cup (260 g) natural Greek-style yoghurt or garlicky whipped tahini (see page 223) onto a serving plate, pile the maple carrots on top and finish with 1 tablespoon each of za'atar and pepitas (pumpkin seeds), a drizzle of pomegranate molasses and a squeeze of lemon juice.

Crispy-skin fish and veggie chips with garlicky butter bean dip

This is a light, tasty riff on the classic fish and chips. If you don't want to pan-fry the fish, feel free to bake it – just choose a fish without skin, lightly oil and season it, then bake in the oven for around 7 minutes. You could also leave out the fish and serve the fries as a stellar snack or side.

4 x 150 g (5½ oz) firm-fleshed fish fillets, such as barramundi, blue-eye trevalla, Spanish mackerel, ling or NZ king salmon

6 carrots, peeled and cut into quarters

4 large parsnips, peeled, cut into quarters and cores removed

⅓ cup (80 ml) olive oil

Sea salt flakes and ground black pepper

1 tablespoon za'atar

Handful flat-leaf parsley leaves, finely chopped

½ lemon, cut into wedges, to serve

Garlicky butter bean dip

1 x 400 g (14 oz) can butter beans, rinsed and drained

1 clove garlic

2 tablespoons olive oil, plus extra to drizzle

¼ cup (65 g) hulled tahini

Juice of ½ lemon

Place the fish fillets on a board, skin-side up. Gently run the back of a knife down the fish's skin to release any moisture, then pat it dry with paper towel. If you have time, let the fish sit in the fridge, uncovered and skin-side up, for at least 2 hours to further dry out.

Preheat the oven to 220°C (425°F) and line a large baking tray with baking paper.

Combine the carrots and parsnips in a bowl and drizzle with 2 tablespoons of the olive oil, then season with a little salt and pepper. Scatter them onto the tray in a single layer and roast for 20–25 minutes, until they are charred and just cooked.

Meanwhile, make the garlicky butter bean dip by combining all the ingredients in a blender with ⅓ cup (80 ml) water and blending into a smooth purée. Adjust the seasoning to taste with salt and pepper, then pour into a small serving bowl and top with half the za'atar and drizzle with the extra olive oil.

Season both sides of the fish with a little salt. Heat a non-stick frying pan over medium–high heat. Add the remaining olive oil, then carefully add the fish, skin-side down. Season the flesh with pepper, then firmly press down on the fish with the back of a spatula for 10–20 seconds. Cover with a lid, reduce the heat to medium and cook for a further 3–4 minutes. This allows the flesh to cook gently and the skin to become very crispy. Keep a close eye on the fish, as the cooking time may vary slightly, depending on its thickness.

Turn off the heat, flip the fish over and let it rest in the pan for 1–2 minutes. Transfer to a plate and keep warm.

Scatter the parsley and remaining za'atar over the veggie fries and serve them with the garlicky butter bean dip, crispy-skin fish and the lemon wedges to squeeze over.

Fennel, potato and leek gratin

Nothing says comfort food like a gratin bubbling away in the oven. Fennel has to be one of my all-time favourite veggies. Raw, pickled, grilled, roasted or in a braise – it can do no wrong. It gives this dish a lighter touch, not to mention a delicious anise flavour. This gratin is delicious on its own or alongside a crispy-skinned fish fillet or a whole roast fish – see below for some suggestions. Add my raw winter slaw (page 200) for some freshness and crunch.

2 large fennel bulbs, cut in half lengthways

1 leek, cut in half lengthways

2 red-skinned potatoes, such as desiree, peeled

¼ cup (60 ml) olive oil

Sea salt flakes and ground black pepper

3 cloves garlic, chopped

1¼ cups (310 ml) single (pure) cream

2 cups (120 g) fresh breadcrumbs

½ cup (50 g) grated gruyere or cheddar

Preheat the oven to 200°C (400°F).

Lay the fennel, cut-side down, on a board and cut into 1 cm (½ inch) thick slices. Cut the leek into 5 mm (¼ inch) thick slices. Cut the potatoes into 5 mm (¼ inch) thick slices.

Place a large frying pan over medium–high heat and add the olive oil, fennel, leek and a good pinch of salt. Cook, stirring often, until the fennel and leek begin to break down and the fennel starts to caramelise, 5 minutes. Transfer to a baking dish.

Add the potato, garlic and cream to the baking dish and mix well. Adjust the seasoning to taste and make sure everything is evenly distributed.

Cover the dish with foil and bake for 45 minutes, then carefully remove the foil, sprinkle with the breadcrumbs and cheese and return to the oven for a further 10–15 minutes until golden.

Pro tip Prepare the gratin up to 2 hours in advance and then reheat it in the oven to serve.

Goes with

· Pan-fried ocean trout fillet
· Whole roasted snapper
· Pan-fried ling fillet

Octopus and blood orange with green goddess tahini

I created this dish while I was testing out another recipe for this book. It was a warm winter's day, I had a couple of blood oranges lying around and, thanks to my love of Middle Eastern and Mexican flavours, this dish was born – and has been on high rotation at my place ever since. This makes for a delicious lunch towards the end of winter, when the days get warmer and blood oranges burst into season. If you want to make this at other times of the year, just use regular oranges.

1 kg (2 lb 4 oz) cleaned octopus

1 small brown onion, cut into wedges

2 cloves garlic, crushed

Sea salt flakes and ground black pepper

2 tablespoons olive oil

¼ cup (60 ml) Everything Mexican marinade and dressing (see page 225)

Juice of 2 limes

3 blood oranges, peeled and cut into 1 cm (½ inch) cubes

½ small red onion, finely chopped

Handful coriander (cilantro) leaves, chopped

1 tablespoon coriander seeds

1 tablespoon sesame seeds

1 tablespoon extra virgin olive oil

½ cup (130 g) green goddess tahini sauce (see page 222)

Place the octopus in a saucepan with enough water to completely cover them. Add the onion, garlic and 1 teaspoon salt and bring to the boil, then reduce the heat to low. Place a heatproof plate over the octopus to ensure they remain submerged, and cook for 35–40 minutes, until just tender. Transfer to a bowl and allow to cool to room temperature before cutting the octopus into separate tentacles.

Heat a barbecue, char-grill pan or frying pan to high, lightly brush the octopus with the olive oil, then grill for 4 minutes, until lightly charred, turning a couple of times throughout. Transfer the octopus to a heatproof bowl and toss with the Everything Mexican marinade and dressing, and the juice of ½ lime, until combined. Set aside.

Combine the blood orange, red onion and chopped coriander in a bowl and set aside.

Place the coriander seeds and sesame seeds in a small frying pan over medium heat and toast until the sesame seeds are golden and fragrant. Add to the blood orange salsa along with the extra virgin olive oil, the remaining lime juice and a little salt and pepper, and gently mix through.

Serve the octopus with the blood orange salsa and the green goddess tahini sauce drizzled over the top.

Pro tip Cook the octopus and make the green goddess tahini sauce up to 3 days in advance and keep in the fridge. You could also turn this into tacos by wrapping the octopus and blood orange salsa in warm corn tortillas and adding some sliced avocado.

Herb-seared kingfish with buckwheat salad and garlicky whipped tahini

Searing and herb-crusting fattier fish like kingfish is one of my favourite ways to prepare it – see page 29 for more tips. This dish has all the flavours I love – coriander seeds, sumac and garlicky tahini – which all perfectly complement the kingfish. The buckwheat salad gives it body while keeping things light.

500 g (1 lb 2 oz) kingfish fillet

Sea salt flakes and ground black pepper

2 tablespoons olive oil

Handful flat-leaf parsley leaves

Handful dill sprigs, finely chopped, plus extra whole sprigs, to serve

Finely grated zest of 1 lemon, plus 1 lemon, cut into wedges, to serve

1 tablespoon coriander seeds, toasted and lightly crushed

½ teaspoon sweet smoked paprika

⅔ cup (185 g) garlicky whipped tahini (see page 223)

Buckwheat salad

1½ cups (295 g) buckwheat, soaked overnight and drained

Handful flat-leaf parsley leaves, roughly chopped

Handful mint leaves, roughly chopped

2 spring onions (scallions), thinly sliced

1½ teaspoons sumac, plus extra to serve

1 tablespoon chardonnay vinegar

Juice of ½ lemon

¼ cup (60 ml) extra virgin olive oil

Place a non-stick frying pan over high heat and season the kingfish with salt and pepper. Add the olive oil to the pan and sear the kingfish for 20 seconds each side, ensuring the middle is still raw. Transfer to a plate and place in the fridge to cool.

Combine the herbs, lemon zest, coriander seeds and paprika in a bowl. Spread half of this mixture over a piece of eco-friendly wrap and place the cooled fish on top, pressing it gently into the herbs.

Scatter the remaining herbs over the fish to completely cover it, then roll the wrap firmly up and around the fish. Twist the ends to secure them and create a tight log, then return to the fridge for at least 1 hour.

To make the buckwheat salad, bring a saucepan of water to the boil. Rinse the buckwheat, then add it to the boiling water and cook for 4 minutes. Refresh under cold running water, drain it well again and place in a bowl with the herbs, spring onion, sumac, vinegar, lemon juice and extra virgin olive oil. Season to taste and mix through.

To serve, cut the kingfish into 2 cm (¾ inch) thick slices, then remove and discard the wrap. Smear the garlicky whipped tahini over a large plate, place the kingfish on top and spoon the buckwheat around the kingfish. Sprinkle with a little extra sumac and the extra dill sprigs, and serve with the lemon wedges.

Raw winter slaw

This bowl of goodness is on my table at least once a week during the cooler months, because it's so quick, delicious and nourishing. Sometimes, even in winter, you just want a crisp fresh salad. Feel free to swap in veggies like shaved brussels sprouts or broccoli.

This slaw can share the table with so many other dishes, or hold its own as a light casual meal. I serve it with any fish, fillets or whole. If you're making this for 1–2 people, you'll be able to enjoy it a few more times.

1 small fennel bulb, trimmed and cut in half, fronds reserved

4 small silverbeet (Swiss chard) leaves, thinly sliced

¼ radicchio or chicory, thinly sliced

¼ small white cabbage, thinly sliced

4 radishes, sliced into thin rounds

Handful mint leaves, roughly chopped

Handful dill sprigs, roughly chopped

2 spring onions (scallions), sliced

Sea salt flakes and ground black pepper

2 tablespoons chardonnay vinegar or apple cider vinegar

⅓ cup (80 ml) extra virgin olive oil

½ cup (50 g) shaved parmesan (optional)

Finely shave the fennel using a mandolin or a sharp knife and place it in a large bowl. Add the silverbeet, radicchio or chicory, cabbage, radish, mint, dill and spring onion and toss to combine. You can prepare this up to 2 hours in advance and refrigerate until you're ready to serve.

To serve, season the salad with a generous pinch of salt and a good crack of black pepper. Add the vinegar, olive oil and parmesan (if using) and toss everything together well.

Goes with

· Grilled Spanish mackerel fillet
· Crumbed hake fillet
· Roasted whole mirror dory

Istanbul fish sandwiches

I first tried this sandwich over 10 years ago during my travels through Turkey. It's served up many different ways depending on who's making it, but at its heart, it is unfussy and totally delicious street food. The fresh hit of herbs and tomato, and the zingy pomegranate molasses and sumac, all give your tastebuds a punch. Try to use a light crusty roll, like the ones your local Vietnamese bakery sells. Ciabatta would also work. This sandwich is best made with richer fish like blue mackerel or even bonito, but I've also made it with mirror dory, bream and rainbow trout.

1 tablespoon pomegranate molasses
Juice of ½ lemon, plus extra
¼ cup (60 ml) olive oil
½ teaspoon sumac
Sea salt flakes and ground black pepper
1 small red onion, thinly sliced
4 x 120 g (4¼ oz) blue mackerel fillets
¼ iceberg lettuce, thinly sliced
Handful dill sprigs, roughly chopped
Handful mint leaves, roughly chopped
4 long crusty bread rolls, cut in half
2 vine-ripened tomatoes, sliced
4 large or 8 small store-bought pickled chillies (optional)
⅓ cup (90 g) sumac yoghurt (see page 223), optional

Preheat a barbecue, char-grill pan or large frying pan to high.

In a bowl, whisk together the pomegranate molasses, lemon juice, 2 tablespoons of the olive oil, the sumac, salt and pepper. Add the onion, stir through and allow to stand at room temperature to macerate.

Season the fish with salt and pepper and drizzle with the remaining olive oil, then grill or fry it, skin-side down, for around 2 minutes. Flip the fish over and cook for 1 minute, then transfer to a plate and spoon a little of the pickling liquid from the onion over the top to keep it moist.

Combine the lettuce and herbs in a small bowl with a squeeze of lemon juice.

Toast the buns, cut-side down, on the hot barbecue or pan. Top the bun bases with the lettuce and herb mixture, then follow with some tomato, the fish and the pickled onion, spooning any reserved pickling liquid over the top. Finish with the pickled chillies and sumac yoghurt (if using) and tuck in.

Turmeric fish, coconut and chickpea curry

This curry is so nourishing and comes together so quickly. Make the turmeric paste in advance, as you can keep it in the fridge for up to a month and use it in soups, broths or turmeric lattes. You could also stir it through some natural yoghurt and use it to marinate fish or veggies. This recipe can easily be adapted to become plant-based – just swap the fish for some roasted eggplant (aubergine), cauliflower or pumpkin (squash), and throw in some extra greens.

2 tablespoons olive oil

1 small brown onion, finely chopped

2 cloves garlic, finely chopped

Sea salt flakes

1 vine-ripened tomato, chopped

400 ml (14 fl oz) vegetable stock

1¼ cups (310 ml) coconut milk

1 x 400 g (14 oz) can chickpeas, rinsed and drained

500 g (1 lb 2 oz) firm white-fleshed fish, such as ling or hake, cut into 3–4 cm (1¼–1½ inch) pieces

1 bunch English spinach leaves, roughly chopped

Handful coriander (cilantro) leaves, roughly chopped

Juice of 1 lime

Steamed rice or quinoa, to serve

Turmeric paste

¼ cup (60 ml) coconut or olive oil

¼ cup (40 g) ground turmeric

1 thumb-sized piece ginger, peeled and sliced

1 teaspoon ground cinnamon

½ teaspoon ground black pepper

To make the turmeric paste, place all the ingredients in a blender or food processor with ⅓ cup (80 ml) water and blend until smooth.

Transfer the paste to a small saucepan and cook over medium heat for 5–7 minutes, whisking until it is reduced and thick. Reserve half the paste in a bowl, then pour the rest into a jar or container, allow to cool and store in the fridge for up to 1 month.

To make the curry, heat the oil in a saucepan over medium–high heat and add the onion, garlic and a good pinch of salt. Cook for 3 minutes, stirring often, then add the chopped tomato and cook for a further 3 minutes to break it down. Add the reserved turmeric paste and stir through. Pour in the stock, reduce the heat to a simmer and cook for 4 minutes.

Tip in the coconut milk and chickpeas and bring to the boil, then add the fish and gently poach it for 5 minutes. Add the spinach and carefully stir through until wilted.

Scatter the coriander leaves over the curry, squeeze some lime juice over the top and serve with the steamed rice or quinoa.

Mussels with nduja, chickpeas and gremolata

Mussels are the ocean's fast food and should be on every home's weekly menu. They're super affordable, sustainable and nutrient-dense, and can be on the table in under 30 minutes. They're also really versatile and adaptable to many flavours. This dish works with any legumes, such as white or butter beans.

¼ cup (60 ml) olive oil

¼ small fennel bulb, chopped

½ small brown onion, chopped

2 cloves garlic, sliced

Sea salt flakes

80 g (2¾ oz) nduja (see Notes)

1 cup (250 ml) white wine

1 x 400 g (14 oz) can cherry tomatoes

1 x 400 g (14 oz) can chickpeas, rinsed and drained

2 kg (4 lb 8 oz) black mussels, scrubbed and debearded

Handful flat-leaf parsley leaves, roughly chopped

Handful basil leaves

Crusty bread and lemon wedges, to serve (optional)

Gremolata

1 large clove garlic, finely chopped

Handful flat-leaf parsley leaves, finely chopped

Zest of 1 lemon

Place a large saucepan over medium–high heat. Add the oil, fennel, onion, garlic and a pinch of salt and cook, stirring, for 5 minutes, until the vegetables soften.

Add the nduja and continue to cook, stirring, for 2 minutes, then pour in the white wine and cook for 1 minute. Add the tomatoes and chickpeas, reduce the heat to a simmer and cook for 5 minutes. Add the mussels, cover with the lid, turn the heat up to high and cook for around 5 minutes, gently shaking the pan until they open. Remove the pan from the heat and give everything a good stir to ensure the mussels are well coated in the sauce.

To make the gremolata, combine all the ingredients in a bowl.

Serve the mussels topped with the gremolata and herbs, with some crusty bread and lemon wedges, if desired.

Notes Nduja is a spicy, spreadable, fermented sausage (otherwise known as a flavour bomb) originally from Calabria in Italy. Find it at some supermarkets and delis or online. If you can't find any, some finely diced chorizo will work, or you could add a pinch each of dried chilli flakes and sweet smoked paprika instead.

Smoky butter beans with fish and rice

There is something truly magical about one-pot cooking – it screams comfort and nourishment, and you always feel like you're winning when producing flavour so effortlessly. This recipe uses the poaching technique on page 33, which is one of the gentlest ways to cook fish. It's perfect if you're just starting out, and is great for small kitchens, as you don't need much room and there are less smells sticking around afterwards. Just remember to season your sauce before adding the fish.

¼ cup (60 ml) olive oil

1 small brown onion, finely chopped

1 small red capsicum (pepper), finely chopped

2 cloves garlic, sliced

Sea salt flakes and ground black pepper

1–2 tablespoons fire-roasted chilli salsa (see page 225), or use store-bought chipotle in adobo

2 teaspoons sweet smoked paprika

1 tablespoon ground cumin

1 cup (200 g) basmati or long-grain rice

1 x 400 g (14 oz) can crushed tomatoes

800 ml (28 fl oz) vegetable or chicken stock

500 g (1 lb 2 oz) skinless boneless ling fillet, or any other firm white-fleshed fish, such as blue-eye trevalla, hake or snapper

1 x 400 g (14 oz) can butter beans, rinsed and drained

Handful flat-leaf parsley leaves, roughly chopped

Handful mint leaves, roughly chopped, plus extra whole leaves to serve

2 tablespoons extra virgin olive oil

Juice of 1 lemon

1 tablespoon za'atar (optional)

½ cup (130 g) natural Greek-style yoghurt

Place a large shallow casserole dish or frying pan over medium–high heat and add the olive oil, onion, capsicum, garlic and a good pinch of salt and pepper. Cook, stirring often, for 4 minutes, until the vegetables are soft, then add the fire-roasted chilli salsa or chipotle, the paprika and cumin and stir through. Cook for 1 more minute, then add the rice, crushed tomatoes and stock, and bring to the boil.

Reduce the heat to a simmer and cook the vegetables and rice for 6 minutes, stirring often, until the rice is partially cooked.

Lightly season the fish with salt and pepper, then nestle it in the vegetables and rice. Give the pan a gentle shake to allow the fish to settle in. Spoon some sauce over the fish, then cover the pan with a lid and cook for around 6 minutes. Remove the pan from the heat and allow the fish to rest for 5 minutes.

Meanwhile, place the butter beans in a bowl with the herbs. Dress with the extra virgin olive oil, lemon juice and a little salt and pepper, and mix to combine.

Spoon the butter beans and dressing around the fish. Sprinkle with the za'atar (if using), and serve with the yoghurt and extra mint leaves.

Braised leeks with hazelnut vinaigrette

This is a delicious take on the French classic. When leeks are slow-cooked, their flavour mellows, turning sweet and rich. For a completely vegan version, replace the eggs with avocado wedges.

This is great as part of a larger spread, served alongside any fish dish and my caramelised cauliflower salad with dates, almonds and buckwheat (page 182).

2 leeks, cut in half lengthways

2 tablespoons olive oil

⅓ cup (80 ml) red wine vinegar

½ cup (125 ml) vegetable stock

Sea salt flakes and ground black pepper

2 free-range eggs

1 tablespoon seeded mustard

¼ cup (60 ml) extra virgin olive oil

1 tablespoon baby capers, rinsed and drained

⅓ cup (50 g) hazelnuts, toasted and lightly crushed

Handful dill sprigs, roughly chopped

Preheat the oven to 190°C (375°F).

Cut each leek half in half again crossways, so that you have eight pieces in total. Place them in a deep baking tray, cut-side down, and add the olive oil, half the vinegar, the vegetable stock and some salt and pepper. Cover the tray with foil and roast for 35–45 minutes, until the leeks are very soft. Allow to cool to room temperature.

Meanwhile, bring a small saucepan of water to the boil, add the eggs, reduce the heat to a simmer and cook for 8 minutes. Refresh the eggs under cold water and peel them. Separate the whites from the yolks, then roughly chop the egg whites and crumble the yolks.

Drape the leeks, cut-side up, over a serving plate, and lightly season them with salt and pepper.

Whisk together the mustard, remaining vinegar, the extra virgin olive oil and capers and spoon half this dressing over the leeks. Top with the hazelnuts, egg whites and yolks, then drizzle the remaining dressing over the top and serve topped with the dill sprigs.

Goes with

· Seared tuna fillet
· Grilled ocean trout fillet
· Pan-fried mirror dory fillet

One-tray roast fish with brothy white beans, capers and lemon

This is delicious no-fuss cooking, perfect for a quick lunch or dinner. If you don't have a sauté pan that can go in the oven, just spoon the brothy beans into a baking dish, then top them with the fish.

⅓ cup (80 ml) olive oil, plus extra to drizzle

½ small leek, chopped

4 cloves garlic, sliced

2 sprigs rosemary

4 anchovy fillets (optional)

¼ cup (45 g) capers, rinsed and drained

Sea salt flakes and ground black pepper

Finely grated zest and juice of 1 lemon, plus 1 lemon extra, cut into wedges

¼ bunch kale leaves, thinly sliced

1 bunch broccolini, cut into shorter lengths

2 cups (500 ml) vegetable stock

2 x 400 g (14 oz) cans cannellini (white) beans, rinsed and drained

Handful flat-leaf parsley leaves, roughly chopped

600 g (1 lb 5 oz) blue-eye trevalla or other firm white-fleshed fish fillet, skin removed

⅓ cup (115 g) 3-minute romesco sauce (see page 222) or salmoriglio (see page 224)

Preheat the oven to 200°C (400°F).

Place a large ovenproof sauté pan over medium–high heat. Add ¼ cup (60 ml) of the olive oil and the leek, garlic, rosemary, anchovies (if using), capers and a pinch of salt. Cook, stirring, for 3 minutes to soften the leek and break down the anchovies, then add the lemon zest, kale and broccolini and cook until the kale is slightly wilted, 1 minute. Add the stock and cannellini beans and bring to the boil, then stir through the parsley and lemon juice. Season to taste with a little salt and pepper.

Place the fish in a shallow bowl, season with salt and pepper and drizzle with the remaining olive oil to coat it. Nestle the fish in the brothy beans and place the whole pan in the oven for 6 minutes, until the fish is just cooked.

Spoon the 3-minute romesco sauce or salmoriglio over the fish and serve with the lemon wedges and a drizzle of olive oil.

Gnarly roasted cabbage with green goddess tahini and spiced pearl couscous

Of all the vegetables, cabbage undergoes the most profound transformation when roasted. It softens and sweetens in the oven, turning meaty and juicy, while its flavour intensifies. The more charred (or gnarly), the better.

1 small white cabbage, cut into eight wedges

⅓ cup (80 ml) olive oil

Sea salt flakes and ground black pepper

1 cup (265 g) green goddess tahini sauce (see page 222)

1 tablespoon za'atar

Pomegranate molasses, to drizzle (optional)

Pearl couscous salad

250 g (9 oz) pearl couscous

¼ cup (60 ml) olive oil

2 tablespoons sherry vinegar

1 teaspoon sumac

1 teaspoon ground cumin

¾ cup (95 g) slivered almonds, toasted

½ cup (85 g) golden raisins, roughly chopped

½ preserved lemon, skin finely chopped, flesh discarded

¼ cup (40 g) pepitas (pumpkin seeds), lightly toasted

3 handfuls roughly chopped herbs, such as flat-leaf parsley, coriander (cilantro) and mint leaves

Preheat the oven to 210°C (410°F) and line a large baking tray with baking paper.

Brush the cabbage wedges on their cut-side with the olive oil and season well with salt and pepper. Place in a large frying pan and cook over medium heat to caramelise each side, then transfer to the tray, cover with foil and roast for 45 minutes. Remove the foil and cook for a further 15 minutes, until they are soft and gnarly.

Meanwhile, cook the pearl couscous in a saucepan of boiling water for 12 minutes. Drain, refresh under cold water and drain well again. Combine with the remaining salad ingredients, reserving half the herbs to garnish, and season to taste.

Serve the pearl couscous salad topped with the cabbage, the green goddess tahini sauce and za'atar. Scatter the remaining herbs over the top and drizzle with a little pomegranate molasses, if desired.

Pro tip Cook the cabbage ahead of time and simply reheat it when needed.

Goes with

· Pan-fried barramundi fillet
· Grilled gemfish fillet
· Whole roasted rainbow trout

Red lentil and coconut dhal with fish

Dhal has to be one of my all-time favourite dishes. I love to top it with roast veggies or seafood to make it even heartier. Feel free to cook the dhal separately to the fish and serve it as part of a larger spread. For a plant-based version, serve it with some roasted cauliflower or eggplant (aubergine) instead of fish.

⅓ cup (80 ml) coconut oil

4 sprigs fresh curry leaves

Sea salt flakes and ground black pepper

1 brown onion, finely chopped

2 cloves garlic, crushed

3 cm (1¼ inch) piece ginger, peeled and finely chopped

2 tablespoons curry powder, plus 2 teaspoons extra

2 tomatoes, finely chopped, or 2 tablespoons tomato paste (concentrated purée)

2 cups (410 g) split red lentils

6 cups (1.5 litres) chicken or vegetable stock

1 x 400 ml (14 fl oz) can coconut milk

2 large handfuls roughly chopped kale or baby spinach leaves

400 g (14 oz) Spanish mackerel fillet, skin removed, or any other firm white-fleshed fish, such as ling or blue-eye trevalla

2 tablespoons olive oil

2 handfuls coriander (cilantro) leaves

Steamed basmati rice or naan bread, to serve (optional)

Heat the coconut oil in a large shallow ovenproof frying pan over medium–high heat. Add half the curry leaves and cook for around 2 minutes, until crisp and translucent. Transfer to a plate, lightly season with salt and set aside.

Add the onion, garlic and a good pinch of salt to the coconut oil and cook, stirring, for 4–5 minutes. Add the ginger, the remaining curry leaves, the 2 tablespoons of curry powder and the tomatoes and cook for 1 more minute, then add the lentils and stir through.

Pour the stock into the pan and cook over low heat for 20 minutes, until the lentils are cooked and creamy. Tip in three-quarters of the coconut milk and cook for 2 minutes, then add the kale or spinach and stir through until wilted.

Preheat the oven to 200°C (400°F).

In a shallow bowl, combine the fish with the extra curry powder, some salt, pepper and the olive oil, until coated. Nestle the fish in the dhal, transfer to the oven and bake for 10 minutes, until just cooked.

Remove the dhal from the oven, scatter with the coriander leaves and drizzle with the remaining coconut milk. Top with the fried curry leaves and serve with the steamed rice or naan, if desired.

ARSENAL OF FLAVOURS

Salmoriglio
Page 224

Zhoug
Page 224

Everything Mexican marinade and dressing
Page 225

Fire-roasted chilli salsa
Page 225

Smoked chilli and
tamarind sauce
Page 228

Green goddess
tahini sauce
Page 222

Gochujang
dressing
Page 228

Garlicky
whipped tahini
Page 223

3-minute romesco sauce

You can absolutely roast your own capsicum (pepper) for this recipe, which is a great idea when they are in season and abundant. But for a no-fuss, max-flavour sauce that you'll want to use on everything, here's my go-to version using store-bought roast capsicum.

Make a large batch of this romesco ahead of time, as it freezes well. It's perfect with any seafood or vegetables, in sandwiches or with eggs in the morning.

Makes 1½ cups (500 g)

200 g (7 oz) good-quality store-bought roast capsicum (pepper)

2 cloves garlic

100 g (3½ oz) toasted hazelnuts or almonds (see Note)

2 tablespoons tomato paste (concentrated purée)

2 teaspoons sweet smoked paprika

2 tablespoons red wine vinegar

Pinch of chilli powder

½ cup (125 ml) olive oil

Sea salt flakes and ground black pepper

Place all the ingredients in a food processor or blender and blend into a chunky sauce. Season to taste. Transfer to an airtight container or jar and store in the fridge for up to 1 week.

Note You can use any nuts or seeds you have on hand for this sauce.

Green goddess tahini sauce

This is a great way to turn forgotten herbs into something zingy and amazing. Feel free to use any soft herbs you like.

Makes 1½ cups (400 g)

Handful coriander (cilantro) leaves, roughly chopped

Handful flat-leaf parsley leaves, roughly chopped

½ cup (135 g) hulled tahini

Juice of 1 lemon

2 cloves garlic, finely crushed

Sea salt flakes and ground black pepper

Place all the ingredients into a blender with ⅔ cup (170 ml) water and blend into a smooth sauce. Adjust the water and lemon juice until you have a smooth consistency. Transfer to an airtight container or jar and store in the fridge for up to 1 week.

Garlicky whipped tahini

This is my everything sauce – I literally spoon it over everything from fish to a tray of roast veggies. It also makes a killer dip and is a great vegan replacement for yoghurt. I love this sauce as it is, but you could add so many other flavours to it like chilli, spices, miso – it really is that versatile.

If your sauce is too runny, just add some more tahini. If you make this by hand, your tahini might look like it has split or it may clump together, but that just means it needs more water and whisking. For a lighter version, make this in a blender.

Makes 1¼ cups (350 g)

½ cup (135 g) hulled tahini
Juice of 1 lemon
2 cloves garlic, finely crushed
Sea salt flakes and ground black pepper

Place all the ingredients in a blender with ⅔ cup (170 ml) water and blend into a smooth paste. Adjust the water and lemon juice until you have a silky consistency. Alternatively, combine the ingredients in a bowl with a whisk or fork, whisking in the water slowly until smooth and combined. Transfer to an airtight container or jar and store in the fridge for up to 1 week.

Pro tip This sauce thickens when stored overnight, so to thin it out again, add lemon juice, water and seasoning as required.

Sumac yoghurt

This is the perfect no-fuss, make-ahead sauce to have on standby in the fridge. Sumac has such a wonderfully fresh, fragrant, slightly sour flavour that really livens up dressings, salads and fish. You'll find so many uses for this sauce – I use it throughout the book. You could also thin it out with water and drizzle it over salads. Try stirring through some chopped fresh mint and grated cucumber and serving it as a dip.

Makes 1¾ cups (480 g)

1½ cups (390 g) natural Greek-style yoghurt
2 cloves garlic, crushed
1 tablespoon sumac
Juice of 1 lemon
2 tablespoons extra virgin olive oil
Sea salt flakes and ground black pepper

Combine all the ingredients in a bowl and season to taste. Transfer to an airtight container or jar and store in the fridge for up to 1 week.

Salmoriglio

This herbie sauce (otherwise known as your best friend) is the flavour of Italy's south. Use it as a dressing, marinade, or spooned over fish. Traditionally, it's teamed with swordfish, but any fish, seafood or roast veggies would work wonderfully. I also stir it through yoghurt, spoon it into soups, or use it to marinate fish in before roasting or char-grilling, finishing with some more sauce after cooking. It also makes a knockout pasta sauce – see page 56 for more.

Makes 1⅓ cup (330 ml)

2 cloves garlic, finely crushed

1 bunch oregano, leaves picked

Large handful flat-leaf parsley leaves

Juice of 2 lemons

200 ml (7 fl oz) extra virgin olive oil

Sea salt flakes and ground black pepper

Place all the ingredients in a blender or food processor and blend into a rustic sauce that's not too emulsified – you want it loose.

Alternatively, use a mortar and pestle to pound the garlic and herbs into a paste, then mix through the lemon juice and oil and season to taste. Transfer to an airtight container or jar and store in the fridge for up to 1 week.

Pro tip Always have this in your fridge. No kitchen should be without it!

Zhoug

Every culture has their own green sauce but for me, zhoug has the edge, thanks to the unique addition of cardamom.

This Middle Eastern version of chimichurri, if you will, injects a huge burst of flavour into dishes and – with help from your trusty blender or food processor – is ready in 5 minutes. Have this in the fridge and you will use it for everything from marinating and dressing veggies and fish, to swirling through soups or spooning into tacos, wraps or sandwiches. It also gives hummus and yoghurt a great kick. The heat from the chilli mellows over time but if you want it a little milder, remove the seeds from the chilli beforehand.

Makes 1 cup (250 ml)

½ bunch coriander (cilantro), leaves picked and some stalks reserved

½ bunch flat-leaf parsley, leaves picked and some stalks reserved

1 long red chilli, sliced

2 teaspoons ground cumin

1 teaspoon ground caraway

½ teaspoon ground cardamom

½ teaspoon sweet smoked paprika (optional)

½ teaspoon sea salt flakes

Juice of ½ lemon

⅔ cup (170 ml) olive oil

Place the herbs, chilli, spices, salt, lemon juice and half the olive oil in a blender or food processor and blend to chop the herbs and chilli, then increase the speed to finely chop everything.

Add the remaining olive oil and pulse to combine, leaving some texture remaining. Transfer to an airtight container or jar and store in the fridge for up to 1 week.

Fire-roasted chilli salsa

There is a little bit of work involved in this recipe, but it's worth it. Double the quantities to make a large batch, as it lasts a while in the freezer, and you'll be pulling it out to enjoy with just about everything. If you prefer a milder salsa, cut the chillies in half lengthways and remove the seeds before grilling them.

Makes 2 cups (500 ml)

6 long red chillies
1 brown onion, peeled and cut into six wedges
2 red capsicums (peppers), deseeded and cut into quarters
3 cloves garlic, roughly chopped
1 teaspoon sea salt flakes
1 teaspoon dried oregano
1 tablespoon sweet smoked paprika
1 cup (250 ml) olive oil
100 ml (3½ fl oz) red wine vinegar

Preheat a barbecue or char-grill pan to high.

Grill the chillies and onion for 5 minutes or until they're a little charred but not too far gone, then transfer to a bowl to cool.

Grill the capsicums, skin-side down, until deeply charred. Transfer to a separate bowl and cover with a clean tea towel or plate so they continue to steam. Once they have cooled, peel and discard the burnt skin.

Roughly chop the chillies, onion and capsicum and place in a saucepan over medium heat. Add the garlic, salt, oregano, paprika, olive oil and vinegar, reduce the heat to a simmer and cook for 5 minutes, stirring often.

Allow to cool, then use a blender or food processor to blend into a purée. Transfer to an airtight container or jar and store in the fridge for up to 1 month.

Everything Mexican marinade and dressing

This is the only Mexican marinade you need in your arsenal – that's how delicious it is. I marinate fish and prawns in this before char-grilling or roasting them for tacos. I also love to brush this onto charred corn, whole roasted cauliflower, eggplant (aubergine), pumpkin (squash) and carrots.

Makes 1½ cups (375 ml)

1 tablespoon raw cacao powder
½ teaspoon ground cinnamon
2 teaspoons ground cumin
1 teaspoon ground coriander
1–2 tablespoons honey or maple syrup
¼ cup chipotle in adobo
½ cup (125 ml) olive oil
¼ cup (60 ml) apple cider vinegar
Juice of 1 orange
1 tablespoon soy sauce
2 cloves garlic

Place all the ingredients in a blender and blend into a purée. Adjust the seasoning to taste, if desired. Transfer to an airtight container or jar and store in the fridge for up to 1 week.

Miso butter
Page 229

Crispy roast chickpeas
Page 230

Babaganoush
Page 229

3-minute romesco sauce
Page 222

Macadamia and lemon myrtle dukkah
Page 231

Lemony crushed butter beans
Page 230

Sumac yoghurt
Page 223

Smoked chilli and tamarind sauce

This sauce hits so many high notes with its hot/sweet/sour/salty magic. It's both a marinade and a dressing, ready to boost any seafood in a flash. It's also delicious spooned over roasted eggplant (aubergine), as a stir-fry sauce, or in curries, broths or noodle dishes.

Makes 1 cup (250 ml)

⅓ cup (80 ml) tamarind concentrate (*see Note on page 156*)
2–3 tablespoons chipotle in adobo
2 tablespoons fish sauce
¼ cup (60 g) shaved palm sugar (jaggery)

Place all the ingredients, with ⅓ cup (80 ml) water, in a blender and blend until smooth. Transfer to an airtight container or jar and store in the fridge for up to 2 months.

Gochujang dressing

Gochujang is on high rotation in our kitchen. The fermented chilli paste is a pantry staple, and a key to creating deliciousness with whatever I have on hand. This dressing has the most amazing, spicy, umami-rich flavour, making it the perfect marinade or glaze. Add this to soups, toss it through noodles or use it to marinate and dress prawns (shrimp) or squid. It's a delicious dipping sauce for sashimi, too.

If you can't find gochujang, you can substitute with equal quantities of white miso and sriracha combined together. For a milder version, you could just use miso on its own.

Makes 1 cup (250 ml)

¼ cup (60 ml) gochujang (*see Note*)
2 tablespoons soy sauce
2 tablespoons sesame oil
2 tablespoons rice vinegar
2 tablespoons honey or maple syrup
2 tablespoons toasted white sesame seeds
3 cm (1¼ inch) piece ginger, finely grated (optional)

Combine the gochujang, soy sauce, sesame oil, vinegar, honey or maple syrup and sesame seeds in a bowl and stir to make a smooth sauce. Add the ginger (if using) and mix through. Transfer to an airtight container or jar and store in the fridge for up to 2 months.

Note Gochujang is a fermented rice-based chilli paste that is popular in Korean cooking. Find it in the Asian aisle of some supermarkets and at most Asian grocers.

Pro tip If you keep your gochujang in the fridge, bring it to room temperature before mixing it with other ingredients, otherwise it will be too hard.

Miso butter

This is the holy grail of flavoured butters. It is amazing melted over whole roast fish, grilled split prawns, seared scallops or in a pot of mussels. Game over!

You could also try it spooned onto whole roast sweet potato (kumara) – just split the sweet potato open and spoon it over; nothing else needed. Same goes for roast cauliflower, cabbage or eggplant (aubergine). It's also delicious tossed through pasta with some squid or prawns (shrimp) – there's endless inspiration!

Makes 1 cup (310 g)

150 g (5½ oz) unsalted butter, softened
2–3 tablespoons white miso
½ teaspoon sweet smoked paprika
1 clove garlic, crushed
Juice of 1 lemon
Ground black pepper
Splash of sriracha chilli sauce (optional)

Bring the butter and miso to room temperature, then place in a bowl with the paprika, garlic, lemon juice, pepper and sriracha (if using). Mix well.

Spoon the butter mixture onto a sheet of baking paper and roll into a log, using the baking paper to wrap it. Twist the ends to secure and store in the fridge for up to 1 month.

Babaganoush

Babaganoush is one of the first dips I made as a young kid with my Lebanese-born neighbour. These days, I make it once, sometimes twice, a week. There's nothing quite like the smell and flavour of smoky eggplant. If you haven't made your own before, I encourage you to do so – you really can't beat freshly made baba! Serve this with fish, veggies, bread, or anything.

Makes 2 cups (600 g)

2 eggplants (aubergine)
Iced water
Sea salt flakes and ground black pepper
½ cup (135 g) hulled tahini
2 cloves garlic, finely crushed
Juice of ½ lemon

To serve as a dip (optional)

1 teaspoon za'atar
Extra virgin olive oil, to drizzle
1 tablespoon pomegranate molasses
Small handful flat-leaf parsley leaves or dill sprigs, finely chopped

Cook the eggplant over an open flame or a barbecue preheated to high until the skin is charred and the flesh is soft. Submerge in iced water, peel away the burnt skin and discard. Alternatively, cut the eggplant in half lengthways, preheat the oven to 220°C (425°F) and place the eggplant, cut-side up, on a baking tray lined with baking paper. Drizzle with a little olive oil and season with salt and pepper, then flip them over so they are cut-side down and roast for 15 minutes or until soft. Peel away the burnt skin and discard.

Drain the eggplant flesh on paper towel for 1–2 minutes, then finely chop it. Place in a bowl with the tahini, garlic and lemon juice, season with a little salt and use a spoon to lightly whip it.

To serve as a dip, top with the za'atar, olive oil, pomegranate molasses and a sprinkling of herbs.

Lemony crushed butter beans

These Mediterranean crushed butter beans are the perfect partner to any seafood or grilled veggies. They also make a great dip to smear on toast and serve with my grilled red capsicums on page 96.

Makes 3 cups (750 g)

2 x 400 g (14 oz) cans butter beans, rinsed and drained

⅓ cup (80 ml) extra virgin olive oil

2 cloves garlic, finely grated

Juice of 1 lemon

½ small fennel bulb, finely chopped, fronds reserved

¼ cup (15 g) sliced spring onion (scallion)

¼ cup (5 g) flat-leaf parsley leaves, finely chopped

Sea salt flakes and ground black pepper

2 tablespoons Calabrian chilli in oil (see Note on page 60), optional

Place the butter beans, olive oil, garlic and lemon juice in a blender or food processor and pulse to make a chunky purée. Fold through the fennel, spring onion and parsley and season with salt and pepper. Drizzle with chilli oil, if desired, and top with fennel fronds. Transfer to an airtight container or jar and store in the fridge for up to 3 days.

Crispy roast chickpeas

These chickpeas add so much crunch to salads, thick soups or seafood. They're also a terrific snack on their own.

You can mix up the flavours as you like – think curry powder, miso, maple syrup – anything that offers a smack of deliciousness. Drying the chickpeas well beforehand is paramount.

Makes 2 cups (350 g)

2 x 400 g (14 oz) cans chickpeas, rinsed, drained and dried overnight (see Note)

2 tablespoons olive oil

1 teaspoon ground cumin

1 teaspoon sweet smoked paprika

Sea salt flakes and ground black pepper

Preheat the oven to 210°C (410°F) and line a baking tray with baking paper.

Toss the dried chickpeas with the olive oil, spices and a little salt and pepper until well coated. Scatter over the baking tray and roast for 25–30 minutes, until crisp. Set aside to cool, then store in an airtight container at room temperature for up to 2 weeks.

Note Ensure the chickpeas have been dried very well in the fridge overnight, uncovered, on paper towel.

Macadamia and lemon myrtle dukkah

Dukkah is something I always have in my arsenal. Having flavour and texture bombs like this on hand can take dishes to the next level with minimal effort.

It's so easy to make your own dukkah and you can switch up the nuts, seeds and flavours. Nori (dried seaweed) is a great addition, as are caraway seeds, fennel seeds or nigella seeds.

I use dukkah to give salads, roast veggies or fish that crunch factor. You could also incorporate it into a crumb coating and serve up golden dukkah-crumbed fish with babaganoush (page 229), hummus (page 38) or labneh.

Makes 1½ cups (230 g)

1 cup (155 g) macadamia nuts, toasted and roughly chopped

½ teaspoon ground lemon myrtle

2 teaspoons cumin seeds

2 teaspoons coriander seeds, toasted and lightly crushed

¼ cup (60 g) toasted sesame seeds

¼ teaspoon dried chilli flakes (optional)

¼ teaspoon sea salt flakes

Ground black pepper

Combine all the ingredients in a bowl, mix well, taste and season with more salt and pepper, if needed. Transfer to an airtight container and store at room temperature for up to 1 month.

THANK YOU!

It takes a team. I have so much gratitude for many people I've crossed paths with throughout my life – close and from afar – who have helped me grow and develop, and who have supported and inspired me. You have been my team. Thank you.

To my mum, Elaine; my dad, Brian; and my sister, Kendal. Thank you for the support throughout my life, especially when I was a young apprentice still finding my feet.

To Nadeema, my childhood neighbour and my family (may she rest in peace) – thank you for introducing me to such a beautiful culture, and to food that inspires me to this day.

To my tribe: Cheyenne, Winter, Lake and Cove – you nourish me. Thank you for being my biggest loves, support, inspiration, laughs and motivation, every day. Cheyenne, my beautiful rock, I love you to the moon. Your honesty, patience and care for the kids and me are nothing short of magical. Thank you for being by my side over the last 10 years and for your support while writing this book and through everything else I put my energy into.

To the industry – the cooks and chefs I have worked alongside, supported and been supported by; specifically Chris Whitehead, Hugh Whitehouse, Ry Cunningham and Scotty Mason – you are the head chefs and sous chefs who played pivotal roles in my growth as a young apprentice chef, and who gave me time, support and inspiration, while teaching me discipline.

To my great friend and mentor, Damien Pignolet. Thank you for giving me my first ever head chef role, and for your lessons – not only in food and cooking, but in humility. Thanks also for the encouragement and confidence to develop my own style and tell my story while staying humble.

To John Rankins and Glenda Grice, two amazing humans and friends who took me under their wings at TAFE and mentored me as a young 19-year-old going through a challenging time. John, thanks for travelling with me throughout Australia, New Zealand and then Helsinki to compete on the world stage. I'm so grateful for your selflessness and energy.

To my good friends, Jason Roberts, Itai Leffler and Anthony Gentile – big love, boys. You have been there with me throughout so much in my life, including throughout writing this book during a challenging time in the world. Thanks for helping me clear the mental road blocks that popped up along the way.

Thank you to my manager, Lisa Sullivan, for your support and help in bringing this book from concept to life.

To Jane Morrow and my publishing team at Murdoch Books – thank you for the opportunity to begin telling my story and sharing the deliciousness of my first book. It has been an amazing journey. I admire the process and what it takes to bring this all together.

To the dream team who came together to produce this book – Virginia Birch (VB), Mariam Digges, Tina McLeish, Jacqui Porter and, of course, Lucy Tweed and Rob Palmer, who made the food look even better. Rob – thank you for your magic through the lens.

To the amazing @ChefTomWalton Instagram community – wow, I am blown away by the connection. It's because of you that I keep dishing up the goodness. To see someone on the other side of the world cook my recipes and then share them with their family and friends is the most rewarding and inspiring experience. Thank you for bringing me into your kitchens and letting me be a part of your deliciousness.

To my suppliers – Jason and Frank from GetFish, Craig from Spencer Gulf Kingfish, and Joe at Fruitique Wholesale – thank you for your generous and continued support, well before and all throughout this book.

Finally, to Anthony 'Huck' Huckstep. Mate – thank you for your support and contribution to this book with your articulation and insight into the ever-changing world of seafood sustainability. One of the great things about life – which makes it more interesting and exciting, and really creates strong community – is collaboration and the sharing of knowledge.

**EAT WELL,
TOM**

INDEX

Published in 2022 by Murdoch Books, an imprint of Allen & Unwin

Murdoch Books Australia
83 Alexander Street
Crows Nest NSW 2065
Phone: +61 (0)2 8425 0100
murdochbooks.com.au
info@murdochbooks.com.au

Murdoch Books UK
Ormond House
26–27 Boswell Street
London WC1N 3JZ
Phone: +44 (0) 20 8785 5995
murdochbooks.co.uk
info@murdochbooks.co.uk

For corporate orders and custom publishing, contact our business development team
at salesenquiries@murdochbooks.com.au

Publisher: Jane Morrow
Editorial Manager: Virginia Birch
Design Manager: Northwood Green
Editor: Mariam Digges
Photographer: Rob Palmer
Stylist: Lucy Tweed
Home Economist: Tina McLeish
Production Director: Lou Playfair

Text © Tom Walton 2022
The moral right of the author has
been asserted.
Design © Murdoch Books 2022
Photography © Rob Palmer 2022

We acknowledge that we meet and work on the traditional lands of the Cammeraygal people of the Eora Nation and pay our respects to their elders past, present and future.

ISBN 978 1 92261 616 6 Australia
ISBN 978 1 91166 850 3 UK

A catalogue record for this book is available from the National Library of Australia

A catalogue record for this book is available from the British Library

Colour reproduction by Splitting Image Colour Studio Pty Ltd, Clayton, Victoria
Printed by C&C Offset Printing Co. Ltd., China

OVEN GUIDE: You may find cooking times vary depending on the oven you are using. For fan-forced ovens, as a general rule, set the oven temperature to 20°C (70°F) lower than indicated in the recipe.

IMPORTANT: Those who might be at risk from the effects of salmonella poisoning (the elderly, pregnant women, young children and those suffering from immune deficiency diseases) should consult their doctor with any concerns about eating raw eggs. Please ensure that all seafood and beef to be eaten raw or lightly cooked are very fresh and of the highest quality.

TABLESPOON MEASURES: We have used 20 ml (4 teaspoon) tablespoon measures. If you are using a 15 ml (3 teaspoon) tablespoon add an extra teaspoon of the ingredient for each tablespoon specified.

10 9 8 7 6 5 4 3 2